THE
NEAREST
IN
AFFECTION

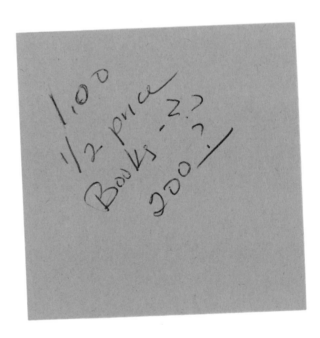

PATHWAYS BOOKS

World Religions: Our Quest for Meaning
by David A. Rausch and Carl Hermann Voss

The Jewish Faith
by Dan Cohn-Sherbok

The Nearest in Affection:
Towards a Christian Understanding of Islam
by Stuart Brown

THE NEAREST IN AFFECTION

Towards a
Christian Understanding of Islam

STUART BROWN

TRINITY PRESS INTERNATIONAL
Valley Forge, Pennsylvania

First U.S. Edition

Originally published by World Council of Churches, Switzerland

Trinity Press International, P.O. Box 851, Valley Forge, PA 19482–0851

Library of Congress Cataloging-in-Publication Data

Brown, Stuart E.
    The nearest in affection : towards a Christian understanding of
Islam / Stuart Brown. — 1st U.S. ed.
       p. cm. — (A pathways book)
    ISBN 1-56338-114-1 (pbk.)
    1. Islam. 2. Islam—Relations—Christianity. 3. Christianity and
other religions—Islam. I. Title. II. Series.
BP161.2.B767 1995
297—dc20   95-6760
                                                        CIP

Cover design: Brian Preuss

Printed in the United States of America

95   96   97   98   99   6   5   4   3   2   1

Table of Contents

Preface

Every year, more than a million pilgrims converge on the dusty Arabian city of Mecca to perform together a series of rituals unchanged in over fourteen hundred years of observance. These pilgrims call themselves Muslims, those who have submitted to the will of God as it was revealed to the prophet Muhammad in these very hills in the early decades of the seventh century CE. From the beginning, there were contacts between the new community and people of Jewish and Christian faith; and the revelations which the prophet received, compiled in the Qur'an, made several references to these other monotheists.

Many verses of the Qur'an have been interpreted to suit arguments at hand, whether to justify caution or to urge friendship. At least one passage, however, is so positive that all readers can agree that the Islamic scripture encourages Muslims to cooperate with Christians in matters of mutual concern:

> You will surely find that the nearest in affection to those who believe are the ones who say, "We are Christians" (Q 5:82).

This text provides the title for this book. Not only does it point to a primordial impulse for Muslims of every age and nation to live in harmony with Christians, but it should also inspire modern Christians to reflect upon their own affection for Muslims in the light of the injunctions of Jesus and the church concerning attitudes and actions of love and peace.

Both Christianity and Islam have found adherents in almost every region of the world, and Muslims and Christians now live together in a great variety of circumstances. Because so much of our shared history has been marked by political and economic rivalry, armed conquest and occupation, few spirits on either side have dared to explore beyond confrontation in search of understanding and common interest. Recent generations, however, have developed a growing respect for the beliefs of their neighbours and a new sense of fairness has fostered more objective descriptions of the teachings and practices of other people of faith.

Enquiring Christians have access to a vast literature covering diverse aspects of Islamic life and thought from a broad range of viewpoints — Islamic, Christian, secular and even from believers in other traditions. The Pontifical Council for

Interfaith Dialogue, the World Council of Churches' Office on Inter-Religious Relations and similar sections for dialogue in regional, national and local ecumenical institutions have encouraged Christians to join in constructive encounter with neighbours of other living faiths, issuing a variety of guidelines, orientations and topical pamphlets to facilitate these conversations.

In many communities, Muslims and Christians have engaged with others in local interfaith organizations whose main agenda has been promoting intercommunal harmony and appreciation of one another's rites and festivals: Vancouver (Canada), Dhaka (Bangladesh), Cairo (Egypt) and Amsterdam (Netherlands) are just a few examples. A growing number of Christians have experienced profound encounters in faith with people of different beliefs, and many of them have participated in a WCC-sponsored study of the theological discoveries emerging from this. Every few months there is a new account of how some individuals from a particular branch of the Christian family have been enriched through interaction with Muslims: two instances are recent publications by the East African YMCAs and the Presbyterian Church (USA).

But our purpose here is not to compile an exhaustive review of the literature on Christian-Muslim relations, which would in any case be out of date before it could be printed. Nor is it to offer a quick course in comparative religion or the dynamics of dialogue — subjects that deserve careful and specific attention in both academic and communal contexts. It is nevertheless true that Christians everywhere face similar types of questions in considering their interfaith attitudes and comportment, and this is especially so in the case of Christians who live among Muslims. Whatever particular circumstances govern the immediate setting — in Nigeria or Pakistan, Tanzania or Texas — the churches together must articulate a common idiom to discuss the theological, diaconal and pastoral challenges posed by the complexities of a plural society in an age of rapid communication and voluminous information.

Whether there can be a single valid Christian view of Islam is hardly the point; it is essential for today's Christians to hear one another in patience and to learn from one another in love as we seek fresh insights which can clearly address the temper of our times while remaining true to the timelessness of the gospel. This little book is one venture in the exploration of a few of the salient issues, as they have been posed by Muslims and Christians in every region of the world. While I have built on my responses to the questions and concerns which I have heard, it is my hope and intention to contribute to a continuing conversation, and therefore to prompt some reflection, to provoke some action and to promote some new measure of serious interaction between the members of the world's two largest communities of faith.

This book is woven from the insights of a few dozen classrooms and the lessons of several hundred conversations in more than fifty different countries; and it would be futile to try to recall everyone's name. Charles Adams and his colleagues at McGill University's Institute of Islamic Studies provided basic information and gentle guidance, while ʿAbd al-Rahman Abu Zayd, Murtada Naqib, Qasim Murad and other Muslim classmates instilled a sense of hospitality which was soon reinforced by friends in Tunisia and Nigeria, especially the late Muhammad Ahmad al-Hajj and my office-mate Nur al-Kali. Later, I was privileged to work with such pioneers in interfaith communication as Wesley Ariarajah, Smail Balic, ʿAbd al-Hakim Tabibi, Michael Fitzgerald and Tarek Mitri. To all (including scores unnamed), I am deeply grateful for both their wisdom and their patience.

My greatest sense of obligation is to those who have shown the most resolute hope in a variety of difficult circumstances, because without their courage in the face of adversity I may not have found the temerity to persevere with an essay of such a positive bent. Here I remember the leaders of the Protestant Student Association of Abdullahi Bayero College (Kano, Nigeria), the Pastoral Council of the Apostolic Mission Church in Burkina Faso, the many participants in the multifaith discussions of Senegal and, most especially, the staff and associates of the Project for Christian-Muslim Relations in Africa in Nairobi and various national centres.

All these people had endowed me with such a treasury of observations that the process of distilling from it a short book for publication proved to be rather more daunting and almost as long as the gathering. Colleagues in the WCC Publications

Department may have occasionally despaired, but they never relented in their calm insistence, until at last the task was done. I thank them for their timely pleas, which gave the necessary rationale to indulge my avocation when more immediate but less important duties crowded my desk.

Through the swirl of events and the tides of fortune, my family has been a haven of refuge and a sure bearing in uncharted adventure. My wife Margaret has shared fully in every swing of our voyage, ready with suasion and caution in due measure, and each of our offspring has opened special channels of discernment through their own immersion in the communities where we have cast our anchor. For these past joys and the promise of the future I salute them.

Most of all, I am grateful to divine providence, which spurred my spiritual curiosity and stimulated my vision of witness in a world of many faiths. In such a world, people will be free to affirm their beliefs and practise their religions in a climate of true charity, each believer's vocation will be for universal justice and peace, and members of different faith groups will indeed compete with one another in good works. The world is certainly not there yet; nor, indeed, has my own pilgrimage ended with the completion of this book. It is, nevertheless, my humble thank-offering, with all its inevitable errors and shortcomings, for which I alone accept full responsibility. May the words of my mouth and the meditation of my heart be acceptable to the Lord, who is my rock and my redeemer (Psalm 19:14).

Stuart Brown

1. The Essential Beliefs of Islam

A valid appreciation of Islam must begin with awareness of what Muslims really believe and respect for their own sense of religion and holiness. We must eschew the prejudices of the past and avoid forming glib new stereotypes. Such honesty is not just a matter of fair play, but a recognition that any misrepresentation or distortion would impugn our own faithfulness by drawing us into a false testimony about fellow human beings whose motives we are in no position to deny.

We begin, then, with a survey of the principal elements of Islamic teaching as seen from a Christian vantage point. This chapter will introduce the person of Muhammad the prophet, the Islamic scriptures or Qur'an and the "five pillars" which are generally accepted as the actions incumbent on every Muslim in the proper practice of the faith. In Chapter 2, we shall look more closely at the understanding of tradition by which religious authority has been justified among Muslims since the time of Muhammad. Already in these two chapters we shall become aware of the diversity within the Islamic community; and Chapter 3 will offer an overview of the major groupings and branches which have emerged over the centuries among Muslims around the world.

Muhammad the prophet and messenger

For Muslims, Muhammad was the last and greatest of a long series of messengers sent by God to call humanity to a life of submission to the divine precepts for creation. He was born in the religious and commercial town of Mecca, in central Hijaz, on the Arabian peninsula, around the year 570 CE.* His kinsfolk were members of the emerging elite living on the caravan trade between Yemen and Gaza, which was profitable despite the severe climate and topography because it avoided the pirates in the Red Sea.

---

* **A note on dating:** The exact year of Muhammad's birth is unknown; and the Muslim calendar calculates years from the *hijrah*, the date Muhammad founded the original supra-tribal community. In what follows, dates are given according to both the Muslim calendar (AH) and the "Common Era" (CE) reckoning, according to which the *hijrah* took place in the year 622. Because the Muslim calendar is a lunar one, the numerical difference between the CE date and the Muslim year is not constant.

Nearly all the inhabitants of the Arabian peninsula claimed descent from the patriarch Abraham through his elder son Isma'il. According to their tradition, the episode in which God spared Abraham's son from ritual sacrifice had taken place in Mecca. Arabs held that it was Isma'il who lay on the altar, rather than Isaac (Gen. 22:1-14; Heb. 11:17-19). In addition, Mecca was the site of a more recent cult honouring three goddesses reputed to be "daughters of Allah"; and the city's rise to prominence was due in part to the pilgrimages which various tribes and individuals made to the shrine.

Muhammad was an orphan under the care of his uncles, who probably took him with the caravans to Gaza, where he may have met some Christian monks in Sinai. He was a capable trader and became the agent of a wealthy widow named Khadijah, some fifteen years his senior. When he was about 25, they married. While she lived, he wed nobody else. Their daughter Fatimah eventually married her cousin 'Ali, and this couple became the ancestors of the prophet's many descendants.

Around his fortieth year, Muhammad became increasingly conscious of a spiritual thirst which led him to spend long periods in solitary contemplation. Eventually, he encountered God's envoy (presumably the archangel Gabriel), who commanded him to transmit God's urgent message to the people of Arabia. The community of believers gradually gained in numbers, drawing most of its converts from the poorer sections of Meccan society. Perceiving a threat to the religious eminence of the three goddesses (and perhaps to the financial advantages they represented), the Meccan elite generally ignored the new call to righteousness or persecuted those who sought to join the prophet. However, Muhammad's prestige spread throughout Arabia, and in time the leaders of the oasis of Yathrib invited him to become their ruler in order to end years of bitter feuding. This town has since been known as *madinat al-nabi* (the city of the prophet) or simply Medina, for it is there that Muhammad founded the first Islamic state. During the last years of his earthly life, he led the Muslims in a series of campaigns against the aristocrats in Mecca. He finally triumphed and was able to perform a pilgrimage to the shrine at the Ka'bah in Mecca shortly before he died.

Notwithstanding Muhammad's great virtue and his prophetic vocation, he was a mortal, and after imparting the message he had received during a period of just over twenty years he died and was buried in his adopted home at Medina. Muslims revere his memory but they never worship him, and the use of the terms "Muhammadan" or "Muhammadanism", in vague parallel with Christian terminology, is both misleading and offensive. The religion of Muhammad's message is considered by Muslims to be the same as that preached by Abraham, Moses, Jesus and a host of other prophets sent to various peoples. This religion is called Islam; the word literally means "submission", and those who submit are known as "Muslims". Both terms derive from the Arabic root *slm*, and it is entirely consistent with Islamic teaching to say that a person who submits to God's will can expect to find real peace (*salaam*).

The Muslim community did focus a broad range of pious perspectives on the mission and personality of Muhammad. His mission was instrumental in reminding humankind of the proper way to live, and to this end he had the dual role of guide and warner. His primary task was to convey God's message, but he was also the human embodiment of right living. This is why many passages of the Qur'an enjoin believers to obey God and his messenger (e.g. 3:32). The actual experience of receiving revelation left Muhammad's personality untouched, nor could he edit the revelation as it came to him, since it was much older than he. Muhammad received revelation in auditory or visual form, just like Ezekiel and other prophets in an earlier age. An important verse (7:157) refers to Muhammad as *ummi*, which may mean "illiterate" or "gentle", but in any case is understood to show that Muhammad had no formal training for his work as a prophet as well as to refute Christian and Jewish allegations that Muhammad had copied or concocted his revelations.

Muhammad never claimed personal infallibility, and it is most unlikely that he would have wished to be venerated. What was important about him was his call to prophethood, and his only miracle was the transmission of the Qur'an. He had no interest in miracle-working, but he deserved respect because God had chosen him to deliver the divine message. When he died, there was no further revelation. Although the community made provision for the continuation of its political and religious direction, the authorities could only interpret the message received through the mediation of its prophet.

From his first call until the end of his life, Muhammad received revelations at irregular intervals. He also maintained his habit of taking meditational retreats, and he encouraged his followers to engage in ascetic exercises like those of the Christian monks in Sinai. In many aspects of daily life, Muhammad was indeed a model for all believers (Q 33:21), though he was not excessively abstemious: he ate and drank as others and even married more than the prescribed maximum of four wives, having received by revelation a special dispensation, presumably to allow him to make alliances with a number of tribal leaders.

Already during Muhammad's lifetime people began to collect "relics" in the form of items he had owned or touched — in spite of his efforts to discourage the practice. Successive generations have tended to increase the emphasis on the prophet's personality, enlarging his place in Islam from the relatively modest role given him by the Qur'an. Within a little more than a hundred years Ibn Hisham was relating miracle stories, although the Qur'an asserts very clearly that Muhammad worked no miracles. A whole genre of literature, the books of proofs of prophecy, had an important influence on the development of Islamic theology as well as popular piety. One group of miracles illustrated Muhammad's power over demons. When a Jewish priest warned people in a market that the child Muhammad would end the nomads' way of life, he and his nurse escaped the crowd by becoming invisible. At his birth, it was claimed, the light from his mother's womb illuminated castles in Syria and the throne of the ruler of Persia shook. In an idea parallel to doctrines of immaculate conception, Muhammad was said to have come into the world in a natural state of piety which others could attain only through strenuous spiritual effort, and he was even said to have been born without a foreskin, thus dispensing with the need for circumcision.

With or without the miracles, Muhammad was and is the prime role model for Muslims, who seek to imitate his sincerity, his generosity and especially his piety. Later generations would affirm that Muhammad and all God's other messengers were sinless. However, the Qur'an criticizes David for his treatment of Uriah and reproaches Muhammad for misdemeanours such as rejecting a blind man's repeated claims on his attention. Exegetical alibis soon restyled the various offences as "mistakes", on the ground that God would never have chosen a scoundrel to transmit the divine message.

The Qur'anic passage (17:1) about a night journey with God has generally been read as referring to Muhammad. While interpretations of this verse vary, nearly all agree that the event endowed Muhammad with the special privilege of conversation with God, whether or not he actually saw the Creator's face. This question of a mortal glimpsing the eternal was of particular interest to the mystics, or sufis, who had become the pre-eminent current of Islamic thought and practice by the sixth century AH. The Qur'anic presentation of Muhammad in the relatively minor role of messenger, with no reference to his own personality or genius, sees knowledge as coming from outside in the form of statements susceptible to rational understanding. The sufis by contrast emphasized not what Muhammad said but what he was. For the sufis, revelation is not knowledge about God or God's will but awareness of God, not insight but participation, not legal learning or ethical behaviour but the transcendent experience of God's presence. Muhammad is the locus in the world of its sustaining force, and ma'rifah is ultimately a personal identification with Muhammad, who is God's outpost among human beings.

Exaltation of Muhammad spawned several corollary doctrines, like the idea that he was in existence before the rest of creation, in a form similar to the pre-existence of Jesus evoked in John 1:1. Indeed, many of these notions have parallels in Christian and Indian cosmologies, although clear linkages have proved elusive. Muslim mystics revere Muhammad as the mediator of divine truth and the light of heaven for creation in a further match for the role of Jesus in the opening verses of John's gospel (1:3-5). To the mystics Muhammad is the greatest of their number and the Qur'an is the most sublime of divine messages, but in a context which connects faith with proper attitudes rather than right dogma. Over time Muhammad became the mystics' perfect person (insan kamil), as Jesus has always been for Christian mystics. Many sufis claimed to have met Muhammad through visions, disregarding the contrary indications of the Qur'an, and his tomb in Medina became a prime object of pilgrimage. Christians in several traditions are familiar with reports of visions or visits of Jesus, Mary and others, as well as pious journeys to the scenes of Jesus's earthly life, to say nothing of the tombs of apostles and other saintly personages. Other Muslims have seen Muhammad through quite different prisms. One influential portrait for contemporary observers is that of the so-called Islamic modernists, who sought to revive Islamic thinking in the face of European political and cultural encroachment during the closing years of the last century. Early modernists agreed with critics from abroad in decrying the apparent decadence of Islamic societies, but they rallied to the defence of their religion and rephrased teachings in a vocabulary that was intended to guarantee viability in the new global intellectual framework imposed by the self-confident heirs of the Enlightenment. Most modernists argued that Muhammad improved the quality of life in Arabia and enhanced the status of women. Some portrayed him as the human embodiment of all virtues (beauty, truth, purity, vigour, courage) and a unique link, valid for all time, between humanity and God. Others emphasized Muhammad's political, social and moral leadership. More recently, social reformers have taken Muhammad as their prototype, an iconoclast who gave people a new order which was more just and less severe than the Bedouin system it supplanted. He has even been called the founder of the first welfare state.

Although the Qur'an clearly denies any possibility of a mediator between God and any creature, popular Islam has long ascribed to the prophet the functions of an intercessor and advocate for the faithful. This idea, which gained currency during the middle ages, seems to have its origins in an ancient Iranian belief that a propitiator was needed to accept the wrath of heaven for an alienated world; of course, the roles of mediator and advocate have always been essential to the person of Jesus in terms of Christian faith.

Muhammad himself believed that he was the shepherd of the Muslims and would accordingly be the last to enter Paradise. Such a role is more exalted than that of a messenger or agent, and popular piety has gone even further in assuming that Muhammad had his own "treasury of merit" to share with his less virtuous followers. Such authority has inspired the veneration and intercessory prayer of great numbers of Muslims in apparent unconcern for the unequivocal disavowals of the Qur'an.

Although nobody remembered when Muhammad had actually been born, the community gave him a birthday which is now celebrated throughout the Islamic world. The prophet's tomb has become a major object of pilgrimage, and prayers offered beside it are believed to be especially efficacious. Muslims also honour Muhammad's family. This is particularly true of the Shi'ah Muslims, but Sunnis have also been solicitous of the standing of his descendants, who are known as *sayyids* or *sharifs*. A series of dynasties of *sharifs* ruled Hijaz for several centuries; the last of these (Hashimis) helped the European allies destroy the Ottoman Empire but soon lost their kingdom to the Sa'udis before establishing a new monarchy in Jordan. Kings of Morocco are also *sharifs*, and hundreds of shrines in North Africa mark the graves of descendants of Muhammad.

The Muslim scripture

The body of the revelations given to Muhammad is the Qur'an, a noun derived from the root *qr'*, meaning "read" or "recite", and probably related to the very first command Muhammad heard in his earliest revelational experience: *Iqra'*! Recite! (in the name God the creator; Q 96:1). It has often been remarked that the Qur'an is the "systematic" Islamic counterpart of the Christian Jesus (Word made flesh), while Muhammad was the *rasul* or apostle sent to spread the message. Because he was only the vehicle of revelation, it is incorrect to refer to Muhammad as the author of the Qur'an. His role was to transmit an eternal message, mediated through him in "plain Arabic", to those hearers to whom God had given grace to understand.

The narratives and epistles of the New Testament represent a much less direct mode of inspiration than the Islamic understanding of the Qur'an, which could in no way be subjected to textual criticism of the sort now commonplace in Christian hermeneutics. Qur'anic exegesis, or *tafsir*, may take note of the particular circumstances in which a given passage was revealed, but the divine immediacy of the inspiration is never questioned. In practical terms, then, it makes little sense and causes needless injury to try to analyze the Qur'an in a manner foreign to Islamic tradition or to speculate about "sources", given that all Muslims believe in its divine origin.

Belief in a written version of the divine will dated from early Sumerian times; and many teachers, including Zoroaster, spoke of a heavenly record of everyone's destiny. The Qur'an assumes that its hearers are aware of this idea and refers to an eternal text preserved on a golden tablet in Paradise, of which the passages revealed to Muhammad are true but partial transcripts. Without scripture, declares the Qur'an repeatedly (e.g. 98:3), there is no revelation.

The received account of Muhammad's calling bears a strong resemblance to the stories of Moses at the burning bush (Exod. 3-4) or Zoroaster's first inspirational experience. The Qur'an came to Muhammad by a process of revelation called *tanzil*, or sending down. The Qur'an mentions Gabriel and Michael as heavenly messengers. Hebrew prophets also speak of angelic envoys: Tobit refers to Raphael, while Daniel mentions Gabriel (8:16; 9:21), who is also named by Luke (1:26) as the herald of the annunciation to Mary. Qur'anic revelation thus followed the pattern of inspiration familiar to the Hebrew prophets. Muslims believe that all such messages derive from the same eternal Word; the Qur'an mentions the Torah, the scrolls given to Abraham and Moses, the psalms of David and the *injil* or gospel of Jesus.

The Qur'an is for Muslims the ultimate revelation to be drawn from the heavenly book. Its phrases are faithful to the original, but they have been reordered by human intervention, for the present sequence of chapters and verses was established only after Muhammad's death had closed the prophetic era. Nevertheless, Muslims affirm that the text in circulation today contains only those utterances which the prophet transmitted during special moments of inspiration, clearly distinguishable from normal conversation. In keeping with the tradition of specific revelations for various peoples, the Qur'an notes that its verses are in Arabic, but the import of the message is universal and, because it is the final revelation, the Qur'an is implicitly addressed to all humanity. Because the Qur'an is taken to be a revelation from God in Arabic, only the actual Arabic wording is scripture, and opinions have varied over the use of parallel texts in other languages to guide believers in the path of faith.

The Qur'an is about as long as the New Testament. It has 114 chapters, each called a *surah* (pl. *suwar*), a word first used to describe the fragments of revelation received by the prophet. Every *surah* has a conventional title, used as a sort of catchword, and is divided into verses, or *ayat*. There are several systems current for the numbering of the verses. With one exception, *suwar* begin with an invocation of the name of God, merciful and compassionate, which is uttered before any recitation or reading of a portion of the Qur'an. The entire text is arbitrarily divided into thirty roughly equal parts, each of which is read on one day of the holy month of Ramadan, and into seven "stages", one to be read on each day of the week. Neither of these classifications takes any account of topical selection. Twenty-nine *suwar* contain series of disjointed letters which have been ascribed magical or mystical significance by various commentators.

Because the Qur'an is a collation of revelations rather than a theological disquisition, it is possible to infer or derive from its verses the basic elements of Islamic teaching. The nearest approximation to a creed is found in 4:136: "Believe in God and his messenger and the book which he revealed to his messenger and the book which he revealed earlier. Anyone who disbelieves in God and his angels, his books, his messengers and the last day has wandered far astray." We have already considered the place of the prophet in this context, and it is worthwhile to review the other components of this injunction as well:

• The God of the Qur'an is the pre-Islamic Allah freed of all hints of association with anything created. God is the one transcendent creator and upholder of the universe, omnipotent, omniscient and judge of all. When he wants something, he says, "Be!", and it is (36:82). God exists from before the dawn of time and into eternity. He calls creation into being and decides life and death (2:258). God is one, for there is only one God and God has only one nature, shared by nothing else. God is not merely the king of all gods, he is the only God, and because of his divine nature he has no offspring, neither the son which the Christians attribute to him nor the daughters of Meccan mythology. This point is made clear by the short *surah* 112:

Say: He is God, Alone, God the refuge, unbegetting, unbegotten; and there is nothing like him.

Transcendent though he is, this omnipotent God can and often does move the hearts and minds of humankind or intervene in his creation. For example, he helped the Muslims to win the Battle of Badr (Q 8). He causes people to accept or reject Islam, just as he condemned Lot's wife to die an unbeliever (Q 27:57). Several verses remind us that God leads astray whom he will and guides whom he will (e.g. 16:93). The Qur'an is not as sternly predestinarian as these examples might suggest, for it firmly lays responsibility on individuals and indicates that those led astray deserve their fate through their own hardness of heart. God leads astray only the evildoers (2:26) and forgives those who repent and accept guidance (20:82). God knows us because he made us, and he is closer than one's own jugular vein (50:15).

• Angels appear in the Qur'an as God's messengers. They are his creatures, who serve and worship him in several ways. Some bear the throne of God (40:7), others keep records of people's deeds (82:10-12) and still others summon souls when their hour has come (16:28-34). Angels helped the Muslims at Badr (3:124), and there will be angels present on the last day (69:17). Only two angels are named in the Qur'an: Michael (2:92) and Gabriel, the most illustrious envoy, who speaks with Mary, Jesus and Muhammad. There are also devils in the Qur'an, but these are more likely to be sinful *jinn* than fallen angels. *Jinn*, like people, may be believers or unbelievers and expect the same consequences. The chief devil is the angel Iblis or Satan, who refused God's command and is now permitted to tempt human beings from the path of truth.

• Besides Muhammad, the Qur'an refers to twenty-eight prophets by name. Three of these are mentioned in the New Testament — Jesus, John the Baptist and his father Zechariah — and eighteen are named in the Hebrew Bible. The Qur'an implies that many other apostles were sent to diverse nations, most of which rejected the message. Muslims accept all these prophets, even the unnamed, and several biblical episodes have Qur'anic parallels, most notably the story of Joseph in *surah* 12 and the virgin birth of Jesus in *surah* 19. The Qur'an of course rejects any ascription of divinity to Jesus and explicitly denies that the Jews could crucify him (4:156); and although it gives him the titles of *kalimah* (word) and *masih* (anointed), these do not carry the same connotations as they would for Christians, for all prophets are somehow anointed and Jesus, like Muhammad, was a bearer of the word of God.

• The last day is the climax of history when graves will open and the *jinn* and humanity will be judged fit for Paradise or Hell. In Paradise faithful men will praise God and rest on silken couches with their wives of perfect purity and dark-eyed maidens, beside gardens watered by pleasant rivers. The Qur'an makes no promises specifically to pious women except that the wine in Paradise is served by ever-youthful boys. Unbelievers and evildoers will be thrown into the fire of eternal torment. The most direct access to Paradise is martyrdom (57:19); otherwise, one must rely on God's mercy, which can be earned through repentance and right living. Muslims have always set great store by good works, principally observance of the duties prescribed by the Qur'an (prayer, fasting, alms and pilgrimage) and abstention from such evils as wine, adultery and usury.

The Qur'an's rhetorical style has links to the poetic tradition of pre-Islamic Arabic. There are some rhymes and some rhythmic passages, but many verses have neither; and some *suwar* are quite prosaic. The most consistent stylistic quality of the Qur'an is a pattern of shifting stresses, reflected in some translations. Each measured unit must be recited in a single breath, and official reciters have developed several different modes of expression for their work. There are few long stories, but a number of loosely connected scenes; and references to individuals like Abraham or Jesus are dispersed through the body of the text. Some verses seem to be responses to particular issues of concern to the Muslims, and many are injunctions recommending or proscribing particular actions. Apart from commenting on the ephemeral character of the works of humankind, the Qur'an makes no historical references beyond the contemporary life of the Muslim community and a solitary mention of the Persian victory over Byzantium (30:2). The Qur'an is not a textbook, but a source book for worship and pious reflection.

Revelations came to Muhammad over a period of some twenty years. Some were very short, perhaps a single phrase of fifteen words, while others comprised a number of sentences. During Muhammad's lifetime, only a few passages were transcribed, and no attempt was made to assemble the revelations in chronological order. In fact, the prophet is reported to have rearranged some verses (75:16-19) and the Qur'an suggests that he may have forgotten some others (18:23; 87-6). Muhammad is quoted as having said that the Qur'an existed in seven different versions. Because some verses were sent to supersede others and Muhammad continued to receive inspiration until his death, the problem of abrogation (*naskh*) was left to successive generations of interpreters. While some instances are explicit, others have been less clear.

> The unbelievers say: Why was the Qur'an not revealed as a complete entity? This was so we could strengthen your heart in this way, and we have phrased it elegantly (25:32).

> It is a Qur'an which we have divided into parts for you to recite to the people at intervals; we have revealed it by stages (17:106).

For several years after the prophet died, there was no written Qur'an; people simply remembered various revelations. A few verses were probably written down by individuals to help them remember the exact phrasing; and as time passed, more and more passages would be committed to writing. Concern for a reliable compilation increased as the prophet's companions aged and died. Some thirty years after Muhammad's death, four rival texts were in circulation, so the *khalifah* 'Uthman commissioned Zayd ibn Thabit and three others to produce a definitive work. They seem to have done a thorough job. Anomalies due to imprecision in the script were later remedied in more than one wording; but these new variants are not particularly controversial in theological terms and Muslims have always affirmed their confidence in this Uthmanic recension.

Initially some Muslims opposed any formal attempt to interpret the Qur'an through explanation or paraphrase as presumptuous, since the human creature could not hope to improve the word of God:

> He is the one who revealed the book to you. In it are clear verses which are of the essence of the book and others which are ambiguous. Those with deviousness in their hearts will follow the ambiguous, seeking discord and interpretation. Only God knows the interpretation and those who are firmly rooted in knowledge say: we believe in the book; the whole of it comes from our lord and only persons of understanding will heed (3:7).

However, it proved impossible to prevent people from trying to explain revelation, either to abet their personal piety or to promote a partisan cause. Most Muslims found many interpretations to be offensive, and attention focused on the last clause of this verse: "only persons of understanding will heed." Learned Muslims thus became responsible for providing informed commentary on the Qur'an to help the community follow the path of virtue. Arbitrary interpretation (*ta'wil*) gave way to scholarly exegesis (*tafsir*), which developed as one of the major Islamic religious exercises.

To safeguard against abuses of personal interpretation, *tafsir* must be based on rational knowledge and argument. The first two generations of Muslims limited this knowledge to the authority of the prophet or his close companions, but the great number of comments attributed to these unimpeachable sources has made work difficult for later scholars because of the inevitable ambiguities and apparent contradictions. Early *tafsir* showed no effort at systematic theology. It was recognized that the Qur'an had many aspects, and a person's reputation as an exegete depended on the range of material collected rather than any expository analysis. Almost none of these early works survived, and all were eclipsed by the compilation of Muhammad al-Tabari (d.923/310).

The first serious students of Muslim scripture in Western Europe were Peter the Venerable and Robert of Ketton, who formed a team in Toledo in the mid-twelfth century to translate the Qur'an into Latin. The earliest English version was the 1649 volume edited by Alexander Ross. This was a translation of a French text, however; and the first direct rendering was the careful work of George Sale (1734), along with portions of the noted *tafsir* by Baydawi. Sir William Muir wrote a study of the Qur'an in 1878, but all modern criticism has depended in some way on the comprehensive book produced by Theodor Nöldeke in 1860 and the subsequent publications of his successive disciples. By far the best of this genre in English is the Companion by Montgomery Watt, based on Arberry's version of the text.

The five pillars

The most common watchword of Islam is "*Allahu akbar!*" This is not a "war-cry", contrary to the assertions of numerous propagandists, but a declaration of the kernel of Islamic belief. The literal translation, "God is greater", conveys the exact meaning, for Muslims believe that God is greater — than anything or anyone else — because God is the creator of whatever else may exist. This utter transcendence so suffuses the Islamic awareness of God that the most heinous blasphemy imaginable to a Muslim is the association of any mere creature with the omnipotent, omniscient Creator. Such a rigorous separation excludes any question of incarnation, for divine and human nature are so different that they cannot mingle, and God remains "unbegotten, unbegetting". But God is merciful, and provides creation with the precepts it needs for right living.

The proper practice of Islamic religion is based on five actions or activities incumbent on every Muslim, commonly known as the "five pillars". The first of these is *shahadah*, which can be translated "testimony" or "witness". It is listed first because a person attains official recognition as a Muslim by publicly repeating the twofold declaration that "there is no god but God, and Muhammad is the messenger of God". Readiness to make such an affirmation is universally accepted as the essential act of adherence to Islam. Formal prayers normally begin with the *shahadah*, and it remains the touchstone of faith for believers prevented by imprisonment, persecution or the like from open observance of their other religious obligations. As in Christianity, the ultimate testimony is dying for one's faith; and a *shahid* is a martyr for Islam.

Second, the rhythm of a Muslim's life is marked by regular formal prayers five times a day, starting at dawn when the traditional summons reminds all who hear that "prayer is better than sleep". These prayers may be performed almost anywhere, and are often said in the home or workplace or in simple areas set apart by a ring of small stones, but worshippers always face Mecca as they pray. It is quite in order to pray privately or alone, but much more common to gather in groups behind a leader or *imam*, who sets the cadence for the successive pronouncements and prostrations. It is also customary for believers to assemble at a mosque for the principal prayer on Friday, when a recognized leader will preach a sermon. Muslims wash their hands, feet and faces in symbolic purification before reciting the prayers, which may include, besides formal prayers (*salat*), personal petitions (*du`a*) or praise (*hamd*) whenever they feel so moved. In addition, any new undertaking is preceded by an invocation of the name of God.

Fasting (*sawm*), the third pillar, is thought to help the pious restrain their earthly appetites and focus their spiritual attention on God's mercies and their own service. During the month of Ramadan, Muslims are enjoined to deny themselves food, drink and other forms of physical gratification from the break of dawn until nightfall (exceptions are made for children, travellers and a few others). Many individuals and groups take on extra religious commitments, such as reading through the entire Qur'an. Each evening there are various celebrations, often until quite late, and the end of the holy month is the occasion for one of the Islamic world's major festivals. At other times, individuals may fast for a particular period to fulfil a vow, or simply to deepen their personal devotion.

Fourth, Muslims should, at least once in their lifetime, make a pilgrimage (*hajj*) to Mecca and perform a series of rituals in the company of the faithful from all over the Islamic world. The appropriate moment for this is about two months after the end of Ramadan. Muslims everywhere join the pilgrims in making a sacrifice in observance of their most important feast-day, which commemorates God's provision of a scapegoat to Abraham so that he need not kill his own son. Many Muslims have made the *hajj* several times; others prefer to send relatives or neighbours too poor to pay their own way. In times past, the journey to Mecca and home could take several years, and pilgrims would often have to stop to work along the way, but nowadays governments or charitable foundations hire aircraft to transport the faithful quickly, and the Saudi authorities have developed an efficient system to ensure that all visitors are able to share in the full programme of religious obligations. The lesser pilgrimage (*`umrah*) may be performed at other times, and often entails a visit to the prophet's tomb in Medina.

Finally, it is incumbent upon all Muslims, however modest their means, to provide for those who are less fortunate. Obligatory alms (*zakat*), collected by the government or an appropriate agency for distribution to widows, orphans, the disabled and others in need, are supplemented through private acts of generosity by individual believers. The institution of almsgiving serves to remind everyone that worldly prosperity is actually a transitory gift from God, and each of us has a stake in our neighbours' welfare. In this way, it fosters a deep sense of interdependence, communal solidarity and mutual responsibility.

It is noteworthy that each of these pillars has its counterpart in Christian traditions, although Christians may differ from one another as well as from the Muslims in various details regarding any one of them. Witness to the faith in deed and word is certainly a prime obligation for any Christian. A regular prayer life, both participation in weekly services and private devotions, is an essential part of religious observance in every Christian tradition. Fasting is still important in many Christian communities, and although Christian fasts seldom take the same form as the Islamic practice in Ramadan, their objectives are fundamentally similar. Pilgrimage is also popular among Christians, although they have no obligation to visit any holy places in the manner of the Muslim *hajj*. Almsgiving has always been encouraged within the Christian community, as a matter of conscience rather than a public duty. In no sense, therefore, are the pillars of Islamic religious practice foreign to our own attempts as Christians to affirm and confirm our devotion to the Almighty.

2. Tradition and the Roots of Jurisprudence

One motive for Meccan opposition to Muhammad was the fear that Islam would destroy the traditional culture by undermining the ancient religion and eroding tribal solidarity. To replace the old bonds, Muhammad developed a new sense of community (*ummah*) based on Islam. Even though the history of this community has been rife with rivalry, the ideal survived of a single *ummah* led by one *khalifah* or successor of the prophet. In principle, this *khalifah* would combine religious and political authority in his own person, but only in the capacity of guardian of the prophet's custom (*sunnah*). As he was himself subject to the *sunnah*, the *khalifah* was an executive officer rather than a legislator, although new situations would inevitably call for new ordinances. The constant base of legality was the *sunnah*, derived from the pious traditions concerning Muhammad's deeds and words.

The English word "tradition" generally refers to the complex of institutions which constitute a certain ongoing heritage. In a more restrictive sense, tradition may be a source of knowledge about particular events and techniques; in this sense the word embraces the Arabic concepts of *hadith*, *sunnah* and *ijma'*. Another connotation of "tradition" includes any legendary information, such as comments on the compilation of the Qur'an or the early conquests of the Muslim armies. Transmitted data of this type form part of the overall religious tradition.

The custom of the prophet

Hadith basically means something someone has said, and *sunnah* denotes something somebody has done. In time, *hadith* came to signify a saying of the prophet, passed on by oral report and conveying information useful in relating Muslim thinking to the life of Muhammad. A *hadith* has two parts: a text and a chain of transmitters attesting to the validity of the information. Although it is impossible to discern which parts of the extant *hadiths* are really original accounts of the companions of Muhammad, they are very helpful in tracing the development of theological and social ideas among the first few generations of Muslims. Given that it was originally considered mandatory for *hadiths* to be transmitted orally, it is ironic that the most reliable *hadiths* now available are those which were written down at an early date. Most of the companions had personal notes of their memories of the prophet, which they would consult when telling new or young Muslims about Muhammad.

A *sunnah* is a habit, custom or practice recognized and continued from the past. The term is not confined to the practice of the prophet (*sunnat al-nabi*), but this takes precedence over regional or other customs. The sense of a *sunnah* is the central idea in the Islamic approach to theology; indeed, it sometimes seems to supersede the Qur'an in actually determining the conduct of devout Muslims. In any case, it is through *sunnah* that the Qur'an is interpreted, and *sunnah* has remained the norm for social and individual behaviour in Islamic society just as it was in ancient Arabia.

A *hadith* usually defines some aspect of the *sunnah*, but not every element of the *sunnah* has a supporting *hadith*. Apparent contradictions have not always been explained, and some authorities did not try to test the practicality of their traditions. The *ummah* had great esteem for experts in both law and custom. The concept of *sunnah* was important in setting a proper life-style for Muslims, both individually and as a community. *Hadiths*, on the other hand, were not significant before the second century AH and were surrounded by considerable controversy for another 200 years. It was a relatively simple matter to transform the ancient tribal *sunnah* into an Islamic ideal in conformity with the prophet's own pattern of living. Reverence for his *sunnah* developed at Medina, perhaps during his lifetime; one *hadith* even reports Muhammad as saying that anyone introducing an innovation to his *sunnah* would be accursed. Be that as it may, Medina remained the home of the *sunnah*; and as other countries became interested in applying the *sunnah*, Medina provided the obvious model.

Both the Qur'an and Muhammad had referred to tradition. After the prophet's death tradition became the principal means for the justification of religious authority, far more important than either the charismatic or theistic aspect, even though the Qur'an is always quoted as a basis of judgment. Muhammad never broke with the general norms of Arabian society. His mandate was to command usually recognized behaviour and forbid innovation, except in manifest instances of evil conduct. In other words, Muhammad reintroduced the authority of God into the local tradition; he replaced an ancient *sunnah* with a new one but left society still dependent on a *sunnah*.

At first, the Qur'an was the only arbiter in legal decisions, though sometimes a *hadith* would be mentioned to soften a seemingly harsh punishment. By the second century AH, *sunnah* was gaining more force, and soon it was the virtual equal of the Qur'an. Later still, some scholars suggested that the *sunnah* could abrogate certain verses; and in the fourth century AH, Ibn Qutaybah was ready to argue for the divine origin of the *sunnah*. Where the specific practice of the prophet was unknown, the ways of his companions and other pious ancestors should be adopted. Eventually it became a mark of extreme piety to imitate every known habit and gesture of Muhammad and his companions. Christian history is also familiar with the interplay between tradition and scripture and efforts to live like Jesus or his disciples.

Another key concept, beginning in the second and third Islamic centuries, was consensus or *ijma'*, which still ranks third in importance after the Qur'an and the *sunnah*. Once the *ummah* has resolved a question through consensus, the accepted solution is binding on succeeding generations of Muslims, for Muhammad is quoted as promising that his community would never agree on an error. If a question is resolved in this way, no further personal effort is needed; and by the third century AH the great jurisconsults had established their own consensus, which assumed that all the great issues were indeed solved and future scholarship should be devoted to repetition and not originality.

Contemporary students appeal to the example of the earliest Muslims to justify efforts to apply Islamic precepts to today's circumstances, and the most vehement epithets in Islamic thought apply to innovation. Antipathy to innovation led to rejection of everything which the prophet could not have known — for example, drinking coffee or smoking tobacco. Other conservatives opposed the printing of books and eating with a knife and fork. Such extreme positions could not stop the normal evolution of society, and some innovations were so obviously beneficial or inevitable that they were simply accepted by consensus. *Hadiths* were sometimes fabricated to justify certain novelties (one claimed that Muhammad had approved in advance any good statement by a Muslim). It has been standard practice for new ideas to gain acceptance through consensus on the principle that anything may be tolerated which is not manifestly harmful or contrary to the Qur'an or already established *sunnah*.

By the end of the second century AH, a reaction developed against the wholesale invention of *hadiths*. Paradoxically, new *hadiths* were circulated which quoted Muhammad as condemning the false attribution of statements to him, sometimes in the most apocalyptic terms, such as saying that such a contentious practice would indicate the approach of the last day. Others opposed the whole idea of *hadiths* and condemned the hypocrisy of those who studied *hadiths* they had drafted themselves. Parodies of *hadiths* appeared, and philosophers disparaged *hadith* students.

The need for a methodology of *hadith* criticism became clear as *hadiths* hostile to established *sunnah* became so current that they seemed to threaten the principle of consensus. The first criterion of assessment was the probity of each person in the chain of transmission; the second the inner consistency of the chain of transmission — in other words, was it possible for each succeeding hearer actually to have heard the presumed transmitter? To be sure, it was fairly easy to insert appropriate names and so give health to any particular sequence, and a contest of wits pitted forgers against investigators. Interestingly, only the chains of transmission were scrutinized, and once these were validated the text of the *hadith* was accepted, no matter how absurd its content. If two *hadiths* seemed contradictory, it was necessary to reconcile them or determine which abrogated the other. Affirmative wording took precedence over negative wording. Anachronistic *hadiths* were taken as instances of Muhammad's prophetic gift.

The evaluation of *hadiths* remained more art than science. The only way to learn to assess them with any confidence was to gain a profound familiarity with the corpus. Since there was more interest in questions of law than of ethics or manners, legal *hadiths* were more carefully evaluated. Indeed, there was some encouragement of the fabrication of moral *hadiths*, and the *hadith* which denounced the crafting of lies about the prophet was amended to condemn only falsehoods which would misguide people. Some scholars wrote *hadiths* to reassert the primacy of the Qur'an over *sunnah*. Any worthy maxim could be attributed to the prophet, and there are now *hadiths* in circulation which echo verses of the Bible or old Arabic proverbs.

The roots of jurisprudence

People who have submitted to God and promised to order their lives in conformity with divine precepts could be expected to develop a thorough system to guide and regulate individual and social behaviour in this world. The earliest generations of Muslims did exactly that, elaborating a number of codes of jurisprudence (*fiqh*). Eventually, four prevailing schools emerged, each with its major area of influence but all generally acknowledging the validity of the others. Their differences have little bearing on interfaith relations, so a detailed comparison is unnecessary here, but it is noteworthy that the divergences are much more "legal" than "theological". Once the basic affirmation of God's oneness and Muhammad's apostolate has been uttered, a believer's attention focuses on the obligation to do good and avoid evil, and therefore on the relative merits or disadvantages of any possible action. Because all life is subject to the same divine judgment, Islamic teaching understands political, economic, domestic and religious behaviour as interdependent aspects of a single relationship linking a person to society, creation and God.

Naturally, the primary source of guidance is the Qur'an, given that it is taken to be a verbatim transmission of the Word of God, offered to its hearers precisely to help them follow the straight path. Exegetes have plumbed the nuances of every verse, and each generation continues to study and reflect on the application of the text to particular historical or geographical contexts. In fact, only a relatively small fraction of the Qur'an is susceptible to ethical or legal hermeneutics, and this portion provides the substratum for all Islamic jurisprudence.

Situations soon arose for which the sacred book had no ready solution, and the Muslims turned to the example of the messenger who they believed had been chosen to show them the path of virtue. Since Muhammad had already acted as arbiter and leader of the first Islamic state in Medina, it seemed appropriate to continue to pattern administrative and judicial decisions on precedents he had set. In time, a few collections of these *hadiths* gained wide recognition, and they now stand second only to the Qur'an as a source of law. As we have seen, even the voluminous corpus of *hadiths* did not always seem to offer a solution to every new challenge, so many Muslims added a third yardstick by appealing to the established praxis (*sunnah*) or consensus (*ijma'*) of the community. Because of this diligent observance of received practice, the majority group within Islam adopted the term "Sunni" to include all those Muslims who sought to follow the tradition of the founder and his earliest associates. Some parts of the community eventually added a fourth parameter for canonical decisions: analogy (*qiyas*). For example, the use of loudspeakers to broadcast the call to prayer could be sanctioned by analogy because it extended the effect of an action which was already deemed to be beneficial.

These four standards — Qur'an, tradition, consensus and analogy — came to be known as the "roots" or "foundations" of Islamic jurisprudence, and they continue to frame the practical theology of the vast majority of Muslims today. In this sense, virtually every Muslim is a convinced "fundamentalist", and "liberal modernists" are as eager as strict conservatives to ground their judgments and teachings in the very roots of their faith. Although some Christians might call themselves both "liberal" and "fundamentalist", these terms have come to distinguish two sets of attitudes, and here again we must be wary of misleading parallels between different religious traditions.

While the term *fiqh* is generally applied to the proper study and understanding of Islamic jurisprudence, another word, *shari'ah*, refers to the practical implementation or observance of moral precepts in personal and political life. This word literally denotes the "path" for believers or societies to follow if they would be true to their professed allegiance to God and Muhammad, and all governments are enjoined to provide an environment which allows Muslims to perform their religious duties and encourages every citizen to behave in an upright manner. However, there is no definitive code of *shari'ah*, and each authority must decide for itself how to enforce morality among its subjects.

In every era of Islamic history, in every corner of the Islamic world, a kaleidoscope of options has thus illumined the responses of authorities to the doctrinal imperative. Some rulers have very strictly imposed the most severe interpretations in circulation; others have simply required that no new statute could contradict the teachings of Islam; still others have tried to formulate constitutions to embody *shari'ah* within their jurisdictions. As it is the duty and privilege of every Muslim to learn and obey the law according to conscience, disagreements have often arisen on questions of both policy and application. There is, nevertheless, an overall consensus regarding a number of key elements.

In cases where the Qur'an is clear, there is no room for debate. For example, a Muslim man may marry up to four women, as long as he treats them equally and as long as they are from acceptable faith groups, but a Muslim woman may marry only a Muslim and she may be married to only one at any given time. The requirement of equal treatment has led various countries (such as Tunisia) to foster monogamy; and the circumstances in which either spouse may seek a divorce have been subjected to considerable review in recent years.

Adultery is punishable by death, but it is normally required that the offence should be observed by four adult witnesses. The amputation of a hand for theft is conditional on stringent economic criteria that render it difficult to apply this penalty on a general scale. The interdiction against wine (*khamr*) has been extended to all spirituous beverages, but the only forbidden meat is that of the pig. No categorical agreement has yet emerged as to whether the condemned practice of *riba'* includes all forms of interest-taking or only the more exorbitant types of usury.

Classical Islamic political theory distinguishes among three kinds of state. Lands under Muslim control, where the government rules according to *shari'ah*, are part of *dar al-islam*, the house or realm of Islam. Historically, Muslim rulers in such areas have accorded a protected secondary status (*dhimmi*) to "people of the Book", members of tolerated religions like Christians and Jews. Idolaters — and presumably atheists — are proscribed. Territories where Muslims have been prevented from fulfilling their religious duties are in *dar al-harb*, the house or realm of war. It is the duty of all Muslims to use any appropriate means to redress this situation. Muslim subjects should try to persuade their governors to grant them freedom to practise their faith and, if this fails, should resist such authorities and seek to overthrow them. Muslim rulers ought to intervene on behalf of their persecuted co-religionists in neighbouring areas, diplomatically at first, but by armed force if necessary. Between these two is *dar al-mu`ahadah*, the realm of "covenant". In this zone are the areas ruled by non-Muslims who allow Muslims a relatively free exercise of their obligations.

This model served well for centuries, and the life of Christian and Jewish *dhimmis* in Islamic regions was enviable compared to that of religious minorities in the Christian states of Western Europe under the Inquisition, for example. Many held high office as court physicians or cabinet ministers. The adoption of electoral politics in Turkey, Egypt, Iran and other countries with Muslim majorities has raised afresh the question of minority rights. For example, there has been considerable discussion as to whether a non-Muslim may become president of a "Muslim nation" or hold high office under a Muslim president. Elsewhere, there has been heated public debate over the extent to which *shari`ah* can be observed or enforced in mixed societies like Malaysia, Nigeria or Sudan. At the same time, Muslim minorities are seeking recognition for their rules of inheritance and access to education in a morally acceptable environment. The increasing emergence of fledgling democracy in religiously diverse societies will challenge Muslim leaders to adapt their inherited theories or articulate their more inclusive interpretations, even as the political representatives of other traditions must enunciate their own new responses to the same evolving circumstances.

Jihad means literally "effort" or "struggle". In religious parlance the term refers to the effort which faithful Muslims expend in the service of Islam. From the earliest days, scholars have insisted that the major struggle for any believer should be the inner effort towards spiritual purity. The specific quest for religious discernment is called *ijtihad*, and a Muslim who is recognized as having the gifts and training necessary for such endeavour is a *mujtahid*. But Muslims are also enjoined to serve

Islam by public witness in word and deed and to intercede with hostile or negligent authorities who hinder the proper observance of religion. Thus another related term, *mujahidun* (strugglers), has become familiar through its adoption by the Afghan Muslims who actively opposed the imposition of a Marxist government in Kabul. Armed action, or "holy war", is nevertheless a last resort, and to apply so narrow a definition to such a broad concept as *jihad* is to violate the spirit of Islamic doctrine.

3. Branches of Islam

In considering the various "denominational" groupings which have appeared within the Muslim community, we should note that Islam has neither ordained clergy nor sacraments. Thus there is no sense in which any Muslim could "excommunicate" another without refusing to recognize that person as a Muslim. To be sure, there are cases of such refusals, often in the context of justifying a war against an enemy deemed apostate — for example, the Iranian anathematization of the Iraqi leadership during the Gulf War in 1980 — but the prevalent pattern has been to affirm a sense of Islamic fraternity and a general readiness to identify with all Muslims.

About four-fifths of the world's Muslims adhere to one of the four interpretative schools of Sunnism, or the followers of the "way" attributed to the prophet and his companions. Most of the rest are Shi`is, which means that they belong to the *shi`ah* ("party" or "faction") which supported the claims to leadership of the community by Muhammad's near kinsman `Ali and his descendants. The Sunnis saw the *khalifah* as necessary to ensure the continuing governance of the Muslim state. The Shi`is insisted that Muhammad had indicated `Ali as his successor, using the words "anyone who is my *mawla* is `Ali's". *Mawla* is an ambiguous word which could mean "servant" or "master"; in any case, Sunnis attribute these words to family sentiment rather than a political testament. Christians may recall similar discussions about Peter and the rock of faith. Shi`is also claim that certain verses of the Qur'an support `Ali's succession.

After accepting the first two Sunni *khalifahs* for the sake of peace, `Ali felt cheated by the choice of `Uthman as the third *khalifah*, and when `Uthman was murdered `Ali seized his moment as the obvious heir. But he was falsely accused of complicity in the assassination and was outmanoeuvred in the military campaign which ensued. He died on the battlefield, naming his eldest son Hasan to follow him. Hasan acknowledged the superior force of the Umawi family army and retired on a pension to Medina, where he soon died from poisoning, by Umawi agents or a jealous wife. He named his brother Husayn as the next leader, while the Umawi ruler Mu`awiyyah chose his own frivolous son Yazid to be *khalifah* after him. Husayn gathered a large force in Kufah, but Yazid's troops surrounded and slaughtered the Shi`ah at Karbala on 10 Muharram in the year 61 (10 October 680).

Husayn's death changed the Shi'ah into a religious movement and coloured the whole structure of Shi'i thought. While Sunnis believe that the consensus of the *ummah* is the guarantor of truth, the Shi'ah insists that the *ummah* is right only if it follows the infallible imam. Even if they are a minority, Shi'is claim that the true *ummah* is the group loyal to 'Ali, Hasan, Husayn and their heirs. Some of them would claim a divine status for 'Ali, although most have limited their veneration to human dimensions. Shi'is see Sunnis as "mistaken Muslims" who have not understood the importance of following the prophet's chosen imams, and they call themselves "believers".

One early Shi'i leader, Mukhtar, tried to rally support for Muhammad Ibn al-Hanafiyyah, a son of 'Ali's who was not a grandson of the prophet. Ibn al-Hanafiyyah repudiated Mukhtar, but after he died Mukhtar and others claimed that their hero had been taken into a special occult state (*ghaybah*) and would return in triumph on the Day of Judgment. This is the first recorded indication of an Islamic expectation of a *mahdi*, one rightly guided by God. Such a figure is not mentioned in the Qur'an and does not appear in the *hadiths* for over a hundred years after the prophet's death. Both Shi'is and Sunnis have since proclaimed several *mahdis*, and many still await the advent of their particular candidate, in the manner of Jewish or Christian expectations of a Messiah. Most Shi'is are convinced that an imam will bring true religion to an apocalyptic victory before the end of the world.

Rejecting the concept of predestination, Shi'is say that Muhammad's *ummah* has in fact agreed on error, choosing evil and killing the rightful imams. The suffering of the imams helps to redeem the *ummah* and even the Shi'is are in sin because they did not sufficiently help the martyrs. On the last day, it is the imam who will intercede for loyal Shi'is. It is not difficult to evoke parallels here with the "treasury of merit", popular in Western Europe in the later middle ages, which postulated the transfer of spiritual credits from the saints who had gained paradise to sinners whose deficits were presumably otherwise beyond restitution.

Shi'is have found many references to 'Ali in their "hidden" interpretations of the Qur'an. Consensus is not as important for Shi'is as it is for Sunnis, because the real guardian of the *ummah* is the imam, sinless and infallible, an embodiment of divine light. It was on this question of infallibility that the Shi'ah ultimately broke with the sufis, who claimed that anybody could come to know God. Apart from the veneration of 'Ali and his family, Shi'is differ from Sunnis on such questions as *mut'ah*, a contract marriage which may be set for some years or months or even only a few days. Shi'is make pilgrimages to the sites of the martyrdoms of their imams as well as to their tombs.

After Husayn, the succession passed from father to son. The sixth imam, Ja'far al-Sadiq (d. 765/145), named his son Isma'il as heir, but Isma'il died before his father, who then named another son, Musa al-Kazim as the seventh imam. On the day the eleventh imam Hasan al-'Askari, died in 873/260, his young son Muhammad disappeared, but he later returned as the twelfth imam until he vanished again in 940/329. Muhammad's followers asserted that he was the ultimate imam, now in *ghaybah* until the approach of the Day of Judgment. The late Shah of Iran claimed to have met this hidden imam, while the leaders of the revolution which deposed him in 1979 affirmed that they were acting for the same holy personage.

Because they believe this twelfth imam to be the last, such Shi'is are called Ithna''asharis, from the Arabic word for "twelve". Ithna''asharis form the great majority of Shi'is today. After the occultation of the last imam, they developed their own theology and imamology, reaching a high point in the philosophical theology of Nasir al-Din Tusi (d. 1273/672). In the tenth century AH, a Shi'i order of sufis led by the family of Safa' al-Din gained political control of Iran, transforming that country into the world's only predominantly Ithna''ashari society. Shi'is also constitute the major community around the martyr shrines of Kufah and Karbala in southern Iraq, and important minorities live in Lebanon, Syria, Pakistan and India. With their imam in a state of occultation, Ithna''asharis are led by their *mujtahids*, counterparts of the Sunni 'ulama', who speak for the concealed imam.

Those who supported Isma'il's son Muhammad as the seventh imam (instead of his uncle Musa al-Kazim) came to be called Isma'ilis, or sometimes "Seveners". After Muhammad there were apparently three hidden imams before 'Ubayd Allah al-Mahdi seized control of Tunisia early in the tenth/fourth century. The faithful have always affirmed that ʿUbayd Allah was in fact the true heir of ʿAli and Fatimah, the prophet's only daughter. He founded the Fatimi dynasty and his son and grandson reigned from Tunis as his successors. The fourth ruler, Muʿizz, moved to Egypt when it was overrun by his general Jawhar in 969/358.

When the Crusaders arrived in Syria and Palestine, the Fatimi armies were unimpressive in their efforts to stop them. It was difficult for Fatimi and Sunni chiefs in Syria to bury their differences and work together against the invaders. The Fatimi administration was also hampered by rivalries between African and Turkish cliques. Leadership passed to a new wave of Sunnis, and the Kurd Salah al-Din (Saladin) defeated the Europeans and ended the Fatimi dynasty as well, thus depriving the Ismaʿilis of their political base.

On the death of Mustansir in 1095/488, the prime minister designated Mustansir's younger son Mustaʿli (who happened to be his brother-in-law) as successor; and the heir-apparent, the elder son Nizar, fled from Egypt. Mustaʿli in turn was succeeded by his young son Amir, who was killed in 1130/524 by partisans of Nizar. Amir's son Tayyib kept the loyalty of most of the Mustaʿli party, who also won support among Yemeni Ismaʿilis. Tayyib vanished, and his followers have taught that he and his heirs have been "hidden". They are represented publicly by agents (duʿat), who established a minor state in Yemen which endured for several centuries, sending missionaries to many countries. The most fruitful mission field was Gujarat in western India; and in 1539/949 the leaders moved there. About fifty years later there was a split over the succession between Daʾudis in Gujarat and Sulaymanis in Yemen with a small following in India. Today both groups still thrive in western India, but the Sulaymanis have kept their headquarters in Yemen. There are some 250,000 Mustaʿlis, mostly Daʾudis or Bohras living in their own quarter of Bombay. Bohras have their own mosques and do not normally marry outsiders.

Nizar retained the allegiance of most Ismaʿilis outside Egypt, and Nizaris constitute the largest Ismaʿili group today. Nizar's grandson Hasan proclaimed himself God's representative on earth in 1164/554 and abolished the *shariʿah*. His descendants have continued to lead the Nizaris; and after several generations, the leading household moved to India, where British authorities gave its chief the title of Agha Khan, whose line continues to guide the Nizari or Khoja community. The Agha Khan is called the present imam, because he is here among us, unlike the occult imam of the Ithna''asharis or the hidden imam of the Bohras. Khojas teach that each believer should pay tithes to the Agha Khan and that a visit to the Agha Khan is as important as a pilgrimage to Mecca. Their prayers differ from Sunni or Ithna''ashari worship because they offer homage to the Agha Khan, but they do observe the two major festivals with other Muslims.

Several offshoots of Nizari Islam, like the Gupti faith, tend to mix elements of Hinduism with Khoja religion. One group, the 'Ali Ilahis, believe that 'Ali is divine and regard the Qur'an as partly forged. They have no mosques; they drink wine and eat pork, and they are monogamous and forbid divorce.

Another sequence of Shi'i imams was the Zaydi lineage, which ruled northern Yemen until very recently. Zayd was a grandson of 'Ali's son Husayn. He was killed in a revolt in 739/121. His family did not recognize his elder brother Muhammad al-Baqir, and loyalty to Zayd as the fifth imam has earned his partisans the sobriquet of "Fivers". The Zaydis remained in Yemen, developing a *sunnah* along lines similar to that of the majority. They have generally been more like the Sunnis than like other Shi'is. They oppose the establishment of strict rules of succession and refuse to attribute any mystical powers to the members of the eminent house. The imam must be present and visible, and any imam may be replaced by a more competent usurper. Believers are enjoined to rebel against an unjust imam. From the sixteenth/tenth century, the imamate in Yemen was led by a branch descended from Hasan, but a socialist revolution in this century brought its suzerainty to an end. Zaydis have elaborated a system of jurisprudence based on the Qur'an, the consensus of the prophet's family and the inspiration of the Zaydi 'ulama'. Zaydis accepted many of the classic *hadiths* and they have always discouraged mystical practices.

Besides Sunnis and Shi'is, we should note the egalitarian and very puritan Kharijis, who first withdrew (*kharaju*) from the factional confrontations over political and religious leadership, then sought vainly to mediate, before finally retreating to secure areas on the periphery of the Islamic world, like Oman and the Mzab oases on the fringe of the Algerian Sahara. Kharijis believe that individuals are responsible for their own actions and, therefore, that one's faith can be judged by one's deeds. Sinners deserve to be expelled from the *ummah* and may be killed without penalty by any believer. On the question of leading the *ummah*, the Khariji attitude is unique. Whereas Sunni theory says the *khalifah* should be from the prophet's tribe of Quraysh and Shi'is insist that only his descendants may be imams, Kharijis teach that any Muslim, even someone born a slave, may be recognized as imam.

The chief proponent of the movement for withdrawal from the conflicts and temptation of the central lands was 'Abdallah ibn Ibad al-Murri (d. ca 728/110), and the "moderate" Kharijis are called Ibadis after him. A more vigorous group are the Azraqis, named for Nafi' ibn Azraq, who insisted that sinful Muslims (though not Christians or Jews) should be killed whenever the chance arose. They condemned the Ibadis as sinners for their leniency. The Azraqis disappeared late in the seventh/first century after the failure of an uprising, as did various other Khariji groups. The Ibadi community survived, first in Basrah and later on the southeastern coast of Arabia. During the eighteenth/twelfth century they accepted the leadership of the family of Abu Sa'id, which still rules Oman today. For almost two hundred years the dynasty also reigned over Zanzibar; and Kharijis are still the majority in the oases south of Algiers and on the island of Jarba in modern Tunisia. Other small communities survive in western Libya.

Kharijis believe that reprobate Muslims suffer eternal punishment in hell, while the repentant may hope that the prophet will intercede for them. Because they denounce anthropomorphism, Kharijis are suspicious of the idea of seeing God and oppose mysticism. Loss of purity and, consequently, exclusion from worship result from sinful acts, including lying, calumny, lust, listening to musical instruments and touching a member of the opposite sex who is not a relative. Legal tradition is based on the Qur'an, the *sunnah* and some analogy. The Kharijis have strictly applied the *shari'ah* but they decline to worship with their Sunni neighbours.

The origins of the Druzes, secretive worshippers with their own holy writings who constitute one of the principal faith communities in Syria and Lebanon, go back to Hakim, a Fatimi *khalifah* in Egypt (996-1021/386-411). In keeping with Isma'ili doctrine Hakim saw himself as the active intellect and representative of God on earth. But he surpassed even these parameters in believing that he was actually the divine self. He won several companions to this point of view, notably the Turk Muhammad al-Darazi and the Persian Hamza ibn 'Ali. These two competed for leadership in the movement until Darazi died in 1019/410. Although Hamza's ideas formed the basis of the sect's teaching, the group took his rival's name (*duruz* is the plural form). Their belief that Hakim was an embodiment of God and thus superior to 'Ali and Muhammad is of course rejected by the Isma'ilis and other Muslims. Druzes also ascribed divine attributes to particular leaders of the movement; for example, Hamza was the Intellect and a reincarnation of Adam.

When Hakim disappeared, Hamza said he was in an occult state to test his followers and would soon return. Some months later, Hamza announced that he too would depart but would be back shortly with Hakim. As his successor, he named Baha' al-Din Muqtaná, who encouraged the faithful with a series of epistles over several years. Since Muqtaná's withdrawal from public contact, Druzes have officially refused new converts and told their adherents to prepare for the return of Hakim and Hamza. Religious leadership has continued with a class of 'uqqal or initiates open to anyone who meets seven conditions: never steal or lie except to protect the faith; always be ready to defend other Druzes; renounce other religions; avoid persons of other faiths; recognize Hakim as God; be content with whatever God does; obey God's representatives. For several generations, the supreme shaykhdom has been in the Hajari family of southern Syria. Druzes may marry only other Druzes; they are monogamous but permit divorce. Wine and tobacco are forbidden. During this century the Druzes have been very active in the political life of the eastern Mediterranean.

The Ahmadiyyah movement describes itself as Islamic, but most Sunnis and Shi'is vigorously denounce Ahmadis as perverters of Islam. Ghulam Ahmad (1839-1908/1255-1326), born in Punjab, studied Arabic and Persian, and spent hours in contemplation, during which he heard special voices. In 1889/ 1306 he announced that he had received a revelation from God authorizing him to accept the allegiance of other Muslims. Several people followed him, and two years later he proclaimed himself to be both Messiah and *mahdi*. For the remainder of his life, he continued to receive revelation and perform miracles (including reviving the dead). He claimed to be a reincarnation of Jesus and Muhammad and an avatar of Krishna. The Qur'an (61:6) quotes Jesus as foretelling the mission of a prophet named Ahmad. While most Muslims assume that this refers to Muhammad, Ghulam Ahmad applied it to himself. Noting that the Qur'an (4:156) denies that the Jews killed Jesus, Ghulam Ahmad also taught that Jesus survived his crucifixion and after his recovery moved to Kashmir to tend his lost sheep, eventually dying in Srinagar.

Ghulam Ahmad wrote a book of "Ahmadi proofs" and insisted on full respect for the Qur'an as the supreme scripture, but did not believe that it was the eternal or final revelation. He upheld the five pillars of religion, accepted *hadiths* which could be interpreted to support his case, endorsed polygamy and forbade alcohol and tobacco. He said that he and Muhammad had each been chosen by God as a mirror of the divine image. After Ghulam Ahmad's death, his followers elected as *khalifah* Mawlawi Nur al-Din, who kept the movement together until he died in 1914/1332.

Soon the community split. The majority, calling itself the Ahmadiyyah Movement in Islam, now has over 500,000 members, with half in Pakistan, a quarter in India, large communities in West Africa (especially Ghana) and smaller groups in Indonesia, Britain, the Arab world, America and elsewhere. Its headquarters is in Rabwah, Pakistan. The *khalifah* of the Ahmadiyyah Movement is advised by a council but his decision is final. Ghulam Ahmad is recognized as a prophet, but Ahmadis believe that any of their number could receive new revelation from God. They claim to practise the only true Islam, and Muslims have in turn stigmatized Ahmadis as infidels, conducting severe persecutions in Pakistan, India, Afghanistan and other countries. The Movement supports extensive missionary activity and has a large mosque in London. Ahmadis pay tithes to the Movement and submit internal disputes to their own courts.

The minority who left the Ahmadiyyah Movement established the Ahmadiyyah Society for the Propagation of Islam, based in Lahore. This Society recognizes Ghulam Ahmad as a *mujaddid* or the leader of a religious revival, but denies that he ever claimed to be a prophet: Muhammad was the last prophet and the Qur'an is God's ultimate, perfect book. The Society publishes material on Islam and sends missionaries to Africa, Indonesia, Europe and the USA, but it tends to a "liberal" or "modernist" view of the faith and accepts all who follow Muhammad as Muslims.

Although Baha'is consider their religion to be quite distinct from Islam, Muslims nevertheless reproach them for distorting truth by introducing new material to the received corpus of scripture. In some ways, the Baha'i faith could be said to emerge from an Islamic context in a manner reminiscent of Christianity's birth in a Jewish setting, or perhaps the genesis of the Mormon faith in Christian America.

The apparent spiritual antecedents for this community are among the Shi'is of Iran. Both Ithna''asharis and Isma'ilis spoke of the Bab as the second highest official in the hierarchy after the imam. In 1844/1260, a devout Persian named Sayyid 'Ali Muhammad was first recognized by his friends as the Bab — the gate or door to initiate a new prophetic cycle. Without revealing this mission, the Bab launched a campaign against corrupt religious leaders. The next year he went on the *hajj*. Offended by the moral laxity of his fellow-pilgrims, when he returned to Persia he permitted his followers to declare publicly that he was the mirror of the breath of God. Several dignitaries supported him, but the Bab was arrested and condemned to death in 1847/1263. Seven of his disciples were also killed. His body was later moved to lie in state in a special mausoleum in Acre.

The Bab abrogated several Qur'anic rules about worship, marriage, divorce and inheritance and developed some special spiritual interpretations of terms relating to death, resurrection and judgment. He raised his own home to the status of *qiblah* or focal point for prayers, and he introduced a calendar of nineteen months of nineteen days each, with a four or five-day period at the end of each year; the last of these months was to be the new time for fasting. His regime was lenient, with capital punishment replaced by a system of fines and enforced sexual abstinence. The Bab forbade wine and begging, abolished individual almsgiving and instructed women to discard their veils.

Severely persecuted, few in number and divided, the Friends of the Bab expected a new prophet to come soon. A smaller group, called Azalis after their leader Subh-i Azal, lived by the letter of the Bab's writings. The more numerous section followed an individual who had been among the very first Babis, even though he never met the Bab. His name was Baha' Allah Husayn 'Ali Nuri and his people were called Baha'is. In 1852/1268, while he was a prisoner of conscience in Palestine, Baha' Allah heard a voice summoning him to speak and write. Exiled to Iraq, he won many followers after he claimed in 1863/1279 to be the one foretold by the Bab. He moved to Edirne, where he announced his mission and won the support of most Babis. He was later allowed to settle at Acre, where he died in 1892/1307. The movement split again, this time between Baha' Allah's two sons, with the majority following the elder, 'Abbas 'Abd al-Baha', who travelled widely around Europe and America, founding Baha'i communities. He died in 1920/1338 and was succeeded as leader by his grandson Shawqi Wali Amr Allah.

The Baha'is teach that God is transcendent and unknowable, so they are not interested in mysticism. For Baha'is, the world is eternal because God is in a constant mode of creation. Prophets or divine manifestations are neither messengers nor incarnations but mirrors of God: Adam and the prophets of the Qur'an, Zoroaster, the Bab and Baha' Allah. All prophetic religions are essentially true but the Baha'i faith is the best for this era, which will last half a million years. The Baha'is have a complex teaching about fallen humanity journeying to God through faith. Paradise is a symbol of this voyage. Although religions are essentially the same, one faith is needed to reassert the unity of humankind. Science and religion are in harmony, the sexes are equal and all children are to receive primary instruction. Religion is the key to every social and political difficulty. Baha'is use the Bab's calendar of nineteen months. There are three short prayers to say daily and there is an assembly every nineteen days for listening to the scriptures (Bible, Qur'an or other) and eating a communal meal. The faithful are encouraged to perform a pilgrimage to the Universal House of Justice in Acre. Baha'is may smoke tobacco, but drinking alcohol is forbidden.

* * *

Other, smaller groups have appeared at different times and in various places, but those named here will be the most familiar. Christians engaged in conversation with Muslims should be aware of the broad delineations of these groups, whose complexity of origins and teaching and practice is a reminder of the bewildering gamut of Christian confessions and denominations with their subtle criteria of differentiation. It is important to remember that such systematic classifications tend to represent theoretical models and that any authentic dialogue must stem from the living faith of the participants, which will occasionally diverge from the strict orthodoxy of the texts. In dialogue, we explain our own faith with candid respect and, free from facile stereotypes, seek to understand the beliefs and concerns of our partners as they express them in the same spirit of openness.

4. Points of Contact: Theology and Philosophy

If Muslims and Christians are really to be near to one another in affection, there must be points of contact where this affection may germinate, take root and grow. The meeting-ground between Islam and Christianity is especially rich in theological cross-references, both in the narrow sense relating specifically to God and human awareness of the divine and in the broader context which embraces concepts like revelation and prophecy. Often, however, it is precisely at these theological junctures that differences are most troublesome, and it is sometimes helpful to begin with a common consideration of subjects that are more open to consensus and collaboration, or perhaps a practical discussion of general concerns of a social or political character.

This chapter and the next survey three important areas in which understanding between Christians and Muslims might be fruitfully nurtured — theology, philosophy and (in Chapter 5) the mystical tradition. Rather than contrive extended parallels, which may or may not address the particular circumstances of individual Christians and Muslims, it is more appropriate simply to outline the Islamic experience and to mention the most important historical figures, allowing Christian readers to discover for themselves the junctures at which the insights of faithful Muslims evoke elements of their own tradition and background. Because of radical differences between the two faiths concerning such fundamental concepts as the word of God and the role of Jesus as prophet or redeemer, believers in their respective communities will have divergent understandings of the import of any observation. But many Christians and Muslims can already affirm that their own faith has been immeasurably enriched by their awareness and appreciation of the sense and perspective of neighbours of the other faith.

God, revelation and prophecy

Christians and Muslims believe that God is, and that God is one. They affirm that God created all things and appointed humankind to govern the earth as a vice-gerent. In both traditions, God is called by many names, evoking both God's absolute majesty or power and infinite mercy or grace. God may intervene in the course of human history, whether on the grand scale of world politics, in the minute details of daily existence or even indeed in realms of nature beyond the limits of human competence. God hears and answers the prayers of those who turn to their Maker for help, and God has sent a series of messengers to proclaim the divine will for human beings and all other creatures. God is both immanent and transcendent.

Like Jews and Christians, Muslims regard Abraham as the pioneer of true worship. But they reject two ideas which are essential to Jewish and Christian teaching respectively. God has sent messengers to many peoples, and Moses was one of the greatest of these, but (Muslims will say) God would never choose one nation in preference to all others. It is equally inconceivable to them that a God of utter peerlessness would beget a human offspring (no matter how poetically or metaphorically this is understood by Christians) or allow any mere creature to share in the measureless sovereignty that can only belong to the eternal author and preserver.

The chain of prophets called to exhort humankind to obey the law of God and live in harmony with other people of peace and the rest of creation includes many figures from the Hebrew Bible, beginning with Adam and Noah. The Qur'an mentions other names, unknown in the Bible, and also indicates that some messengers will be remembered only by God. Muhammad is the "seal of the prophets" because he brought the definitive revelation for the entire world, superseding all earlier messages, which had in any case been corrupted in various ways by the communities to whom they had been entrusted. The Qur'an recognizes Jesus as the son of a virgin and as a word (*kalimah*) from God, describes him as working miracles even while a child, and says he will judge his followers on the last day, not according to their adoration of his person, but by their faithfulness to his teachings.

For Muslims, the Qur'an is a transcript from the eternal Word of God as it was dictated to Muhammad by an angel during certain moments in which he experienced a special state of awareness, clearly distinguishable from his normal consciousness so that his own discourse could not be mingled with the revealed Word. As it developed its codes of practice and doctrine, the community would of course give pre-eminence to God's Word and second place to the sayings of the messenger in recognition of his special role. Although a similar distinction between human observation and divine inspiration is made by St Paul (cf. 1 Cor. 7:25), it is not so evident in the Torah and the gospel, because Jewish and Christian scriptures set revelation in a framework of narrative or teaching that seems to muffle the divine utterance in a bundle of contingent words. From the Muslim viewpoint, whatever Abraham, Moses or Jesus said under direct inspiration is of primary interest; what they said themselves is of secondary import; and what others have said about them comes a distant third.

Much has been said on the issue of whether the one God of the Muslims and the one God of the Christians is the same. Some Christian theologians have suggested that while Muslims are correct in supposing that God is one, the Allah whom they worship is only imaginary. Such thinking has its echo among Muslims who argue that it is the Christians who have missed the mark and ought not to call God by the Qur'anic name, Allah. Thus, translations of the Bible which may circulate freely in Indonesia have been banned in Malaysia because of their alleged profanation of terms which have been sanctified by Islamic usage.

However, Christians in Arabic-speaking countries have always used "Allah" in the same way as Europeans have said "God", "Dieu" and the like; and Christians and Muslims who have shared a common language for generations use the same word — for example, "Mungu" in Kiswahili. No creature can claim full acquaintance with a transcendent Creator, and both Bible and Qur'an would seem to allow for a general awareness of God's presence and power beyond the spiritual elite. If interfaith discourse is to have any sense at all, we must hear each other on the understanding that Muslims and Christians alike aspire to serve the one true and living God, however imperfect our respective efforts may be.

Human knowledge of God

Given that we are talking about the same God, our conversations about God's will and God's word will resonate with a common inkling of the pitfalls besetting any human exploration of the unfathomable reaches of theological speculation. Successive generations of theologians in Christendom and *dar al-islam* have been obliged to consider similar mysteries, even if they have applied different methodologies to derive divergent solutions. The range of opinion on such questions as free will and predestination or the limits of divine intervention is equally broad in either camp, though there is a stronger tendency among Muslims than Christians to accept events as part of the unfolding of a divine plan.

That the Qur'an recognizes Jesus as a "word" from God in no way diminishes the sublime respect Muslims owe the Qur'an itself as the most holy of words. They hold that all prophets, including Jesus, have received an identical message of salvation through submission to the divine will, but the Word received by Muhammad (the seal of the prophets) is the final, most complete rendition given to humanity. Nor can the Qur'an's respect for Jesus dilute the reverence which Christians give him as Word made flesh, transcending speech. On a secondary plane, the sayings of Muhammad have an importance to Muslims next to the revealed word, while most Christians have a deep respect for the Bible as "the word of the Lord" which sets the mission of Jesus in its historical and eschatological context. We can learn much from the varying balances between Word and word which our traditions have nurtured.

Indeed, "theology" is an inadequate rendering of the Islamic idea of *kalam*. The roots of the two words and their implications are quite different. The letters *klm* subsume words about speaking, and *kalam* carries the sense of talking about religious faith. Early teachers resisted efforts to systematize religion beyond the Qur'an and *hadiths*. "Talking about religion" was discouraged, and *kalam* was probably first used as an epithet of disapproval. Many scholars held that a subject called *kalam* should be taught only orally. Others explained that the notion derived from the central role played by verbal debate in its initial articulation. As a technical term, *kalam* now applies to the reasoned expression of religion or the attempt to prove the truth of religious belief through argument. The practitioner of *kalam* is a *mutakallim*.

In Islam, as in most other religions, theology is derivative and secondary; and there was a long period when Muslims had no interest in rational exposition of their faith. The Qur'an is not a book of theology; its mode of expression, like that of the most accepted *hadiths*, is not theological. The prophet did not speak from his own reason, but from inspiration, and his message was in dramatic language. The Qur'an sometimes seems to support both sides of a question, such as predestination, but this was probably not a problem for Muhammad, who underlined the imminence of divine judgment and the duty of each person to make a conscious choice to serve God.

The irreligious behaviour of the Umawi rulers of the second century AH provoked the first serious discussion of theological issues after Muhammad's death. A variety of tendencies was emerging within Islam — ranging from the ascetic separatism of the Kharijis, who set up their autonomous realms on the fringes of the desert, to the casual permissiveness of the Murji'is, who deferred religious judgment until the Last Day and recognized as a Muslim anyone who would repeat the *shahadah*. Originating as an attempt to answer unforeseen theological challenges to the *ummah*, *kalam* was a system of apologetics seeking to clarify religious thought and explain the nature of the Qur'an and its own inherent theology, given the apparent juxtaposition of a rigid monotheism and a plurality of names or attributes for God. The process of explaining the sense of the Qur'an also encouraged observant believers to deepen their understanding of the meaning of revelation.

Besides the impulse to comprehend the Quranic message, the first *mutakallims* were moved by simple piety. Hasan al-Basri (d. 728/110) was an ascetic with a mystical bent who formed a group to discuss religion, practise contemplation and undertake exercises of self-denial. The devotion of this company led as well to open criticism of some oppressive governors, but Basri refused to participate in armed rebellion on the ground that God would eventually chastise wicked rulers, even as he used them as agents in punishing the sins of the people.

Hasan al-Basri's position is a clear example of the role played by political difficulties in the evolution of Islamic theology. Another case was the rift over dynastic succession between the Qadariyyah, who upheld the power of human beings to direct their own actions, and the Jabriyyah, who claimed that God caused, even forced, events to occur and that human beings were merely God's agents. If the Umawis were divine instruments, they must be obeyed, but if they were accountable for their own misdeeds, the righteous were under an obligation to remove them from office — in fact, apostasy on the part of a ruler was the only valid excuse for rebellion.

Another religious subject with political overtones was the nature and consequence of sins. There were three points of view. Some said that all sins are intrinsically the same and any sin incurs the penalty of disobedience, which is forfeiture of one's claim to be a Muslim. Sin betrays inner apostasy and should be punished by death. This was the Khariji position. Most Muslims shunned such severity, citing a *hadith* which warned: "If any of you calls someone else an unbeliever, the label should suit either him or you." Others distinguished between major and minor sins, assessing graver consequences for the former. From this perspective, the Umawis had indeed sinned, but so had everyone else, and rebellion was therefore unwarranted. This was the stance of the Sunni majority. Still others maintained political neutrality and preferred to leave judgment to God. This was the point of view of the Murji'is.

The Murji'is also held that faith could be quantified and one person could have more faith than another. This notion eventually gained general currency through consensus. Faith was understood to have three elements: belief, profession and works, pertaining respectively to heart, lips and members. The most important of these was belief, but a believer should show faith by witness and good deeds.

Some verses in the Qur'an (e.g., 18:28) seem to suggest that God will mislead certain people and then chastise them for their offenses, but the Qur'an offers encouragement to both sides of the question of predestination. The weight of *hadiths*, by contrast, was heavily on the side of predestination: not a single one has survived in support of a doctrine of free will. John of Damascus, a Christian student of Islam who lived in the eighth century CE, noted the strong predestinarian stand of his Muslim contemporaries, but Muslim religious thinkers have gradually attenuated the rigours of this attitude. Certain *hadiths* allow that some persons doomed to hell may spend a while doing good and others destined to paradise may experience bad spells, but people will finally establish a general pattern of life in conformity with their ultimate fate.

Arbitrary foreordination may seem inconsistent with the divine mercy and compassion evoked in every chapter of the

Qur'an or even the austere judgment of a person's deeds promised in many passages of revelation. Many serious scholars sought to evade the difficulty by advising Muslims not to ponder the issue too much but simply to accept God's will for themselves. In this mindset, revelation is not only superior to reason but utterly overrides it. These conservatives opposed intellectualism because they wished to maximize the glory of God. Yet a persistent minority always argued that reason is the only vehicle for understanding revelation and God has given human beings reason to help them live in his world. From the earliest ecumenical councils through the debates of Augustine and Pelagius early in the fifth century and the mediaeval discussions of revelation and reason, across the fissures of the Reformation and the craters of the Enlightenment and into the complexities of today's cultural diversity, most Christian traditions have wrestled with quite similar questions of reason and revelation, free will and predestination.

In addition to philology and piety, a third influence on the early development of Islamic theology was the external stimulation of Christian and Irano-Indian ideas about religion, along with the philosophical criticisms applied to all faith. Muslim theologians sought to defend Islam against attacks by Jewish and Christian polemicists, just as Jewish and Christian theologians had earlier sought to refute external threats to their own inherited systems.

Although pre-Islamic Arabia and the Arabic language had no theological or intellectual tradition apart from some heroic poetry, the defenders of Islam adapted the tools and methods of their opponents. Rather than rejecting Hellenistic philosophy, they partially absorbed it. Non-Islamic theologies provided stimulating challenges and a philosophical framework, so *kalam* evolved a vocabulary like that of Christian religious thought. For example, the eternity of the logos was carried into a consideration of the Qur'an as the eternal word of God. Persian influence was also important in the formulation of *kalam*, especially in the assimilation of ancient ideas of dualism into the strict monotheism of Islam. In some regions, Islamic thinkers had to confront such Buddhist notions as the absence of an individual soul and the inexorable change experienced by everything in being.

In seeking to respond to philosophical criticism, Muslim theologians joined the philosophical tradition. For Plato, God was a mythical lawgiver, whose real work was done by wise persons who then ascribed it to divine authorship so that successive generations would respect it. Aristotle tried to demonstrate the logical necessity of an unmoved mover of the universe, the first cause of all movement and existence. Plato had believed it was necessary to invent God; Aristotle tried to prove the existence of God, which Hebrew prophets and early Christian writers, like Muhammad, never questioned, assuming a priori that God was there. But Philo, an Alexandrian Jew, had combined Hebraic and Hellenistic strands to show that Plato and Moses had both been right; and many church fathers had applied their classical education to the task of explaining God and salvation through Christ, while others, like Tertullian and Anselm, attacked the use of dialectic as discrediting the intrinsic purity of the gospel.

This double stream of speculation about the nature of God evoked similar responses from the Muslims when they met it after the conquest of Syria and Egypt. Hellenic paganism had been washed away by the confluence of philosophy and Semitic monotheism, but disagreement persisted about the nature and even the existence of God. The arrival of Islam on the scene simply offered a new variant of the theistic claim for the philosophers to test; and even if the Qur'an seemed to be a straightforward book, those who examined it found many questions susceptible to interpretation and discussion. Islamic fundamentalists, to be sure, denounced this corruption of pristine Islam by the infusion of Greek disputation.

We have seen that the argument about free will and predestination arose within Islam in response to the ungodly rule of the Umawis, but soon the vocabulary and ideas of the old debates between revelation and reason were applied to this issue by the Muslim thinkers who found Qur'anic verses to justify their speculation:

> Call to the way of your lord with wisdom and fair admonition, and argue with them in the better way (16:125).

The verb here translated "argue" was taken as a technical term referring to rational debate, and "admonition" was taken to indicate homiletics. Muslim rationalists identified the wisdom, argument and admonition in this verse with the threefold nature of proof as demonstrative, rhetorical and dialectical, thus offering a divine confirmation of Aristotelian methodology. The philosophers expanded the scope of interpretation to include all aspects of life within God's providence. They wished to submit every aspect of the universe to theological examination, unlike the conservatives, who wanted to assert the supremacy of Islamic law over all creation.

A school of Sunni advocates of freewill known as Mu'tazilis brought elements of rational thinking into the Islamic theological debate. Their five major doctrines were (1) the unity of God in a rather static mode, (2) the absolute justice of God, who would reward or punish people for their actual deeds and not capriciously foreordain anyone to bliss or torment, (3) God's promise that human beings will be treated fairly, (4) the exclusion from the community of only those persons who intentionally commit major sins and refuse to repent and (5) the moral imperative to work for social harmony. After a brief period of ascendancy, this group was supplanted by the theological synthesis developed by Abu al-Hasan 'Ali al-Ash'ari (873-935/ 260-324), himself a Mu'tazili theologian until the prophet came to him in a vision and told him to go his own way. He joined the conservative followers of Ahmad ibn Hanbal, but the prophet urged him to leave them as well, and Ash'ari spent the rest of his career elaborating a middle ground between traditional dogmatism and abstract rationalism, producing the first *kalam* acceptable to the classical religious teachers. The three principal landmarks of Ash'ari's system concern divine attributes, the uncreatedness of the Qur'an and free will.

Recognizing the risks of anthropomorphism in theological speculation, Ash'ari read the Qur'an literally. He insisted that the attributes of God — hands, throne, power, etc. — had to be real and distinct from the divine essence, even if they could not exist without it. But God has these attributes in a different way from humans and without being like humans. So for instance God has power, but not in the same way as people have it. Ash'ari spurned the metaphorical exegesis of the Mu'tazilis and affirmed that people should believe what the Qur'an tells them about God even if they do not understand fully, even if it is impossible to explain, without asking how. Muslims need only know that God is revealed, ineffable Truth, and faith is superior to reason.

The Mu'tazilis had not distinguished between God's word as a divine attribute and the revelation "in plain Arabic" received by Muhammad. This latter was for them the word created by God, while literalists would insist that because the Qur'an was not created, the entire Arabic Qur'an had existed through eternity. Ash'ari distinguished between words of the soul, which are not pronounced, and uttered discourse. God's word has existed from the beginning of eternity but in an unarticulated form, while the revealed Qur'an was created in time. How can the Qur'an be both an unarticulated eternal word and a specific revelation with a created text? Ash'ari answers that one must believe this, without asking how.

In the third place, Ash'ari sought a position between Mu'tazili free will and the rigid literalism of the predestinarians. He criticized a dualism he discerned in Mu'tazili thought: if people are free to do what they choose, they are in a sense creators and thus associates of God. To give people responsibility for their actions, Ash'ari advanced the idea of *kasb*: we receive the power to act from God and by using this acquired power we assume responsibility for our deeds. People are not puppets because they act freely and are thus liable to just punishment for their transgressions. God allows whatever happens but God does not commit evil.

Despite his importance, Ash'ari was not widely followed in his own lifetime. When an Ash'ari school developed, its views sometimes differed from his, because his disciples usually took his ideas to their logical conclusions. For a long time after his death, other schools remained prominent, from the relatively free-will Maturidis of Samarkand to traditional opponents of systematic theology such as the Hanbali jurists. But theological discourse became less important in the Islamic world as it lost political and social relevance. The vacuum this left in popular religion was eventually filled by law and mysticism. In the last century, a new empiricism has brought fresh vigour to theological debates among Muslims and, in a few privileged places, between Muslims and Christians.

Philosophy

Abrahamic monotheism, with its legacy of prophetic messengers and scriptural exegetes, is not the only common heritage of Muslims and Christians. The philosophy of classical Greek schools, especially the followers of Plato and Aristotle, passed from early Christian thinkers to Muslims like Ibn Sina (Avicenna) and Ibn Rushd (Averroes), who in turn influenced medieval European teachers like Aquinas. Given the role of the Spanish Jew Maimonides in this succession, the philosophical corpus of the three Abrahamic faiths is a more closely woven fabric than any other element of our intertwining history. This may have to do with the ambivalent attitude of theologians in all three groups towards those who would serve pure reason, but the fact remains that the same intellectual criteria continue to influence both Islamic and Christian elaborations of the tensions between rational thought and spiritual insight.

Greek thought came to the Arabs through several channels. The emerging Shi`i doctrines of the imamate promoted the idea of an esoteric knowledge passed through the family of the prophet, with the imam as the living vehicle of communication between God and true believers. The Shi`is embraced much of Neo-platonic thought, with its many mystical elements, in their integrated depiction of humanity's place in the universe. Mu`tazilis were sympathetic to the Shi`ah who were more receptive to non-Islamic lines of intellectual endeavour, and the Sunnis who spurned the Mu`tazilis also condemned philosophy. Nevertheless, although the philosophers tended to address non-Qur'anic subjects like the nature of being or the processes of creation, Muslim philosophers were profoundly pious, even if their intellectual stimulation came from outside along an intricate thread of translation from Greek through Syriac and the development of an adequate Arabic lexicon.

The Hellenic heritage provided an amorphous mass of ideas for the Arabs and other Muslims to investigate. Ancient Greeks had been interested in "natural" (physical) science, and both Pythagoras and Aristotle had written on this theme. Medicine, the application of natural philosophy to human beings, had been the special concern of Galen and others, and Ibn Sina would be the heir of this legacy. Plato and his disciples had been preoccupied with politics, the philosophy of the state, and this theme was to be taken up by Farabi. When Muslims began to examine questions of philosophy, Neo-platonism was the dominant tradition among the Hellenistic thinkers, specifically the syllabus of Plotinus and Porphyrus, which tended to fuse or confuse the ideas of Plato and Aristotle. Natural philosophy and metaphysics were the main elements in this trend, but logic, politics and ethics (*akhlaq* or aspects of character) also had their place.

The first Muslim philosopher was Abu Yusuf al-Kindi, an Arab from lower Iraq (796-873/185-260) who sponsored the translation of some 260 philosophical works into Arabic. He was particularly interested in music, mathematics, medicine and metaphysics, and he believed there was a basic congruity between revelation and reason. Kindi defined philosophy as the fullest human knowledge of reality and plumbed the Qur'an for verses to support the case for philosophical research. For example, recalling that the verb "to bow" had a connotation of obedience or worship, he took Q 55:5 ("the stars and trees bow down") as an indication that the universe moves in its own harmony which God has set for it. Philosophers can learn much, perhaps everything, about creation, though only after long and difficult study, but a prophet receives these truths through revelation directly from God.

Kindi passed beyond his Greek antecedents to seek philosophical settings for religious doctrines such as resurrection, which he posited on Q 36:82 — "If God wants something he says, 'Be', and it is." His argument for creation *ex nihilo* followed that of the Syriac Christian John Philoponus, and subsequent Islamic philosophers generally accepted this demonstration, which later appeared in Europe under the pen of William of Ockham. Plato and Aristotle had distinguished between our world and the heavenly world, and many Greeks had identified planets with particular divinities, while Jewish and Christian writers had ascribed angels to the stars. This set the stage for Kindi's interpretation of Q 55:5, already noted. Obedience requires a conscious decision by a rational being, so the stars choose to obey God and the universe responds in harmony to the impulse of its First Cause described by the Greeks.

For Kindi, the goal of philosophy in thought is to attain truth and in action it is to act in truth. Kindi often used the notion of truth to represent God, so it is likely that for him the God of the Qur'an was the philosophers' First Cause. However, Kindi also used the idea of a First Cause to show that human beings are unable to describe God, who is truth transcending all truth. Like Philoponus, Kindi argued that creation had a beginning and would therefore eventually come to an end. Each human soul is a captive within a body but aware of its spiritual origin and therefore in a constant state of unhappiness in the inconstant corporal world. To overcome the sorrows of this changing life the soul turns to reason and science and the exercise of good works.

Muhammad al-Farabi (872-952/259-339), a Turk from Central Asia, studied in Baghdad and spent many years at the Hamdani court at Aleppo before moving to Cairo and then Damascus. Ignoring most of the Neo-platonists, Farabi tried to synthesize Plato's *Laws* and *Republic* with Aristotle's *Ethics* and *Politics* in Islamic terms. Aristotle had said that the supreme aim of human life is happiness (*eudaimonia*), which Farabi equated with *sa'adah* (Q 11:108). His main interests were music and politics; his most original work was *People's Opinions about the Virtuous City*, which argues that there is a natural hierarchy in the universe and nature has endowed the human body with a similar order. The human soul should establish the same order for itself, but this depends on each individual and is not guaranteed. The person or society who would be virtuous will pattern life according to nature's harmony, which is the only valid model for happiness, perfection and justice.

Farabi began by describing the First Cause in terms of God's Beautiful Names in the Qur'an. He posited an astral spirit as the active intellect linked to a human being who has attained maximum development and has thus become the intermediary between the eternal world and the transient world. For Farabi, the active intellect is the Holy Spirit or Gabriel and its linkage with the worthy person is inspiration (*wahy*). Obviously, then, Muhammad is the perfect human, who has attained this privilege of communication with the eternal world through his own intellectual concentration, unlike the revelation which he received through his imagination. The perfect man is both prophet and philosopher.

The greatest medieval Muslim philosopher was Husayn Ibn Sina or Avicenna (980-1037/370-428). Born to a Persian family of civil servants, he was a child prodigy and at the age of 17 became court physician to the governor of Khorasan, but spent most of his life as a counsellor in Isfahan. Ibn Sina was introspective about human nature, starting from the facts of human life and proceeding to the concept of ultimate reality and back to human nature. While his method and structure were Aristotelian, his motives were essentially religious, as he tried to show how everything fits into a divine pattern. For him, contemplation of God was an act of worship.

Ibn Sina rejected the notion of infinite regress and argued for a causal link joining all creation to the unique ultimate reality. Because God is eternal in all his modes, he is forever creating the world *ex nihilo*. Because God's potentialities and actualities are co-eternal, he has only an external relationship with history. Finite beings change with events, but God neither moves nor changes. God is simple, with no agglomeration of potentialities. Because he is a stranger to change, God knows only essences, so he does not hear prayers about particular needs. The resurrection of the dead seemed to imply change in God's eternity, so Ibn Sina questioned the validity of such a doctrine, without explaining why the Qur'an would mention resurrection. Ibn Sina followed Farabi in recognizing prophecy as the doorway to the higher spheres of awareness and prophets as bridges to the First Cause and agents of divine intelligence. The *shari`ah* is the divinely revealed law which Plato had thought should be invented through a myth.

Two or three generations after Ibn Sina, Abu Hamid al-Ghazzali wrote a famous denunciation of the philosophers, effectively ending the Greek philosophical tradition in the eastern Islamic world, but three Spanish writers deserve mention here. Abu Bakr Muhammad Ibn Bajjah (d. 1139/533), who was politically active in his native Zaragoza and later in Fas, wrote several commentaries on Aristotle and closely followed Farabi. Abu Bakr Muhammad Ibn Tufayl (d.1186/581) from Cadiz was a courtier and physician in Granada and Morocco who wrote a philosophical novel about human society and the development of a lone individual to demonstrate that Islamic *shari`ah* as revealed by God is superior to natural law conceived by ordinary mortals. Both these authors were known to medieval European thinkers, but the best-known philosopher of Islamic Spain was Muhammad Ibn Rushd or Averroes (1126-1198/520-595), scion of a famous legal family of Cordova who later became royal physician in Morocco.

Ibn Rushd was a great admirer of Aristotle. His most renowned treatise was a rebuttal of Ghazzali. Ibn Rushd followed Ibn Sina's system of emanations, and he argued against the idea of human immortality or resurrection because form cannot be separated from matter, but he insisted that the *shari'ah* was revealed by God to guide human governance.

After Ibn Rushd's death, few Muslims studied philosophy, but the accumulated Greek and Islamic tradition passed to Western Europe to inspire both Siger of Brabant's so-called Averroism and the work of Aquinas, who followed the traces of Aristotle left by Farabi.

5. Points of Contact: The Mystical Tradition

In addition to scriptural inspiration and philosophy, Islam and Christianity have shared a third mode of discourse about God — mysticism. The book of Daniel, the Apocalypse and the monks of Sinai belonged to the ancient mystical tradition of the eastern Mediterranean, distinct but not isolated from the Celtic heritage of Western Europe and the oriental legacy of Iran and India. In time, a vibrant tradition of Islamic mysticism (*tasawwuf*) fused the lore of the desert fathers with the illuminating inspiration of the people of the East, and its spiritual exercises and individual piety spread to every corner of the Islamic world. This in turn rekindled the mystic ecstasy of the old West among such Christians as John of the Cross and Theresa of Avila. To be sure, the uneasy coexistence of monism and dualism, consuming incandescence and exhilarating enlightenment, fuelled an ongoing debate among both Muslims and Christians, but this similarity in dissent hints again at important conjunctures between the respective frameworks of our structures of perception.

The roots of Islamic mysticism

For Muslim mystics, the starting point was a famous verse from the Qur'an:

> God is the light of the heavens and the earth. The likeness of his light is as a niche in which there is a lamp (in a glass which is like a brilliant star) lit from a blessed tree (an olive neither of the east nor of the west) whose oil would almost shine even if no fire touched it. Light upon light! God guides to his light whom he will. God strikes allegories for people and God knows all things (24:35).

The expressions *sufi* (mystic) and *tasawwuf* (mysticism or mystical practice) are probably derived from *suf*, meaning "wool", in reference to the humble attire of the early Muslim mystics, but the two terms have also been linked to *safi* (pure) and even the Greek *sophia* (wisdom; Arabic *hikmah*). The mystical experience is essentially personal and can be defined only within the parameters of individual relationships with others and attitudes to death. It is easy to repeat heroic phrases and recite sublime prayers but it is quite different to produce these spontaneously.

During the early centuries of Islam, there was little interest in denying the world and the self or in seeking truth or God beyond the context of the Qur'an as God's revealed word. The *sunnah* as the way of life pleasing to God was inferred from the holy book and the recollections of the community about the prophet and his companions. Even so, there were a few Muslims practising ascetic and mystic exercises at a date early enough to indicate that the main source of Islamic mysticism was Islam itself. Nurtured by people of appropriate temperament, this mysticism was later encouraged by contacts with mystics of other faith traditions.

The Qur'an has several verses prompting Muslims to self-denial or ascesis. This present life is likened to water sent from heaven to produce food for people and animals for a while until it evaporates (10:25), or to grass that blooms briefly then withers (57:20). Neither the meat nor the blood of sacrificial animals will reach God, but only the piety of believers (22:37). The Qur'an repeatedly distinguishes between hypocrites and sincere believers and their respective fates (e.g., 2:263-267) and between people who trust in themselves and those who trust in God (18:31-40). And one of its prevalent themes is the awesomeness of the Last Day and the importance of people's actions in deciding their destiny.

There are also verses inviting the pious to inward meditation, including accounts of conversations between God and prophets like Abraham and Noah, the annunciation to Mary, the night journey of Muhammad and the "light" verse quoted above. Finally, there is a special group of verses providing the images used by the sufis to describe their experiences: fire, light, the veils of shadow and light on the heart (41:5), birds as symbols of immortality (67:19), trees representing vocation and destiny (14:24f.) and the promises of paradise (76; 56:12).

Among the companions known to have practised ascetic exercises were Abu al-Darda, who became a Muslim shortly after the Battle of Badr and eventually abandoned commerce to study the Qur'an and contemplate the will of God, and Abu Dharr, an early convert who fasted a great deal to save himself from hardness of heart and is remembered for his dictum that God loves three types of person (those who give secretly to beggars who invoke the name of God, those who pray after a hard night's march and those who are tenacious in combat) and hates three types (those who talk too much, the insolent poor and the cruel rich).

Over the first few generations, the number of ascetics grew slowly but they remained clearly within the norms of the *ummah*, preaching and exhorting both in the streets and in official sermons. Besides attaining a solid reputation as a theologian and *hadith* scholar, Hasan al-Basri (642-728/21-110) was an early exponent of mystical practices. Basri believed that Muhammad had seen God during the night journey and that all believers will see God in paradise. He developed a few rules for a common life, urging his followers to ascesis (*zuhd*), piety and the fear of God. To overcome the apparent conflict between predestination and free will, Basri told people to seek a special mystical condition called *rida*, signifying the mutual satisfaction of the soul and God. Hasan's school continued in Basra for a century, attracting some very pious individuals like Rabi'ah al-'Adawiyyah, a woman who lived to be over eighty (d. 801/185), writing poetry about the love of God based on the conviction that "God will bring a people whom he loves and who love him, humble towards believers, stern to disbelievers and striving in the way of God" (Q 5:54).

The practice of *zuhd* spread from Basra to Damascus and Persia. An Egyptian of Christian background named Dhu al-Nun (796-861/180-246), introduced the idea of stages through which a sufi progresses towards *ma'rifah*, an awareness or unearned intimacy which the Christian mystics called gnosis. In Baghdad, Harith al-Muhasibi (781-857/165-243), a Mu'tazili who had persecuted the Sunnis before his conversion to the sufi path, used his theological vocabulary to articulate themes which are also familiar to Christian mystics and theologians. God made us and may do with us as he pleases, said Muhasibi; our task is to serve God and prepare ourselves for death by renouncing the world. God, who loves the truly faithful, will put love in their hearts. Anyone who does not know God is spiritually sick, and believers who have received God's love have the duty of bringing others to the light.

Abu Yazid Tayfur al-Bistami (d. 974/261), instructed the Indian mystic Abu 'Ali al-Sindi about Islam, learning from his pupil the basic practices of Indian mysticism. Abu Yazid's aphorisms, collected by his disciples, show a strong tendency to monism (e.g., "I left my identity as a snake sheds its skin; then I considered my essence and I was He"). Junayd (d. 910/298), a

Persian student of Muhasibi's and a friend of Abu Yazid's nephew, spoke cautiously of efforts to detach himself from his faculties to attain evanescence (*fana'*) in God. Junayd distinguished the eternal essence from the temporally perceived essence and attributes from actions, thus allowing the believer to be led to a pre-original state within the perceived essence of God. Like Abu Yazid, Junayd followed a spiritual pilgrimage and spoke with God, but his discretion spared him the denunciation of the orthodox, and even won their praise.

Another third-generation Muslim mystic of Zoroastrian antecedents, Husayn al-Hallaj (857-922/244-309), returned to Baghdad after a tour of India and Central Asia and performed public miracles which attracted a large following to his "divine mission". Whereas Bistami and Junayd sought to meet God through ascesis in an ecstasy derived from devout worship, Hallaj used this union with God as a means: through *tawhid* (union with God) persons could be sanctified and even divinized, a state in which whatever they did was quasi-divine, given that they had thus become organs of God.

Such behaviour soon got Hallaj into trouble. Public miracle-working was tantamount to claiming to being a prophet, and his assertion that his acts in the mystic state were somehow divine seemed to put Hallaj beyond the authority of the government. The religious judges condemned his ideas about divine love as polytheistic. Convicted of preaching esoteric dogma, Hallaj was pilloried and jailed for eight years until his friends won a retrial. The second trial, which lasted seven months, ended in a sentence of execution. Hallaj was then beaten, eviscerated, impaled on a cross for a day and finally beheaded for the crime of preaching the love of God and claiming unity, even identity, with this God during a moment of ecstasy ("I am the truth!"). He welcomed his martyrdom as furthering his ultimate *tawhid* but always considered himself to be a Muslim.

Most sufis of Hallaj's time dissociated themselves from his "extremism", and many published their own ideas in order to assuage the misgivings of the religious establishment. The most important mystical author of the tenth/fourth century was Abu Bakr al-Kalabadhi. While referring to Hallaj as a great sufi, Kalabadhi also quoted many legal scholars to appease the authorities. His major work describes methods of attaining spiritual knowledge of God and implies a parallel between the evolution of Sunni law and the development of sufi piety. `Abd al-Karim al-Qushayri (986-1074/376-465) also tried to harmonize *tasawwuf* with Ash`ari theology in a set of two epistles, one addressed to sufis about theology and the other to theologians about mysticism. `Ali al-Hujwiri (d. ca 1075/467), an Afghan living in Lahore, wrote another great compendium of the practices of *tasawwuf*, often lyrical about the ecstasy of *fana'* but insisting that no sufi was exempt from obedience to the law.

Over two centuries, sufis from Dhu al-Nun to Hujwiri elaborated what may be called the "classical" theory or doctrine of *tasawwuf*. The novice sets out on a journey through various stations and successive states, usually seven: repentance, cleansing of the conscience, renunciation of the goods of this world, poverty, longsuffering, absolute trust in God and supreme satisfaction or acceptance of whatever happens. The effort to follow this way is an interior *jihad* which should be undertaken with the supervision of a *shaykh* or guide and involves exercises such as fasting, meditation, prayer, pious remembrance and the examination of conscience. Beyond personal effort one may hope to reach states granted by God's mercy — for example, distant observation, nearness, love, fear, hope, desire, intimacy, tranquil assurance and certitude.

The ultimate goal was union with God, but three distinct concepts of this emerged. Arrival or meeting (*ittisal*) had no hint of identifying the soul with God; union (*ittihad*) meant a natural union and identification; and inhabitation (*hulul*) affirmed that the Holy Spirit dwelt in the purified soul. It is the first of these that the classical authors discussed and the third which Hallaj preached, but it is likely that a great number of sufis believed that they had experienced the second, although they knew better than to say so publicly. But even when they limited themselves to a narrow explanation of *ittisal*, the sufis were still suspected by the religious leaders, who did not see how *ma`rifah* could be possible and believed that human persons could know only what they learned from God through sober study.

The sufis were on better terms with the philosophers, especially Ibn Sina, who was no mystic, but his ideas abetted the development of an "oriental" philosophy that was in fact more mystical than philosophical as these words are understood in Europe. But even Ghazzali, who destroyed Hellenistic philosophy in eastern Islam, considered *tasawwuf* a respectable pursuit for devout Muslims. Ghazzali thought that certain philosophical or mystical truths are beyond the grasp of ordinary folk, and he extolled Muhasibi, Junayd and others as an "intellectual" or "hyper-spiritual" elite whose path he himself sought to follow. Ghazzali set *ma'rifah* above *'ilm* (rational knowledge), but he insisted that mystics must outwardly conform to the same *shari'ah* as everyone else. His mystic teacher was his younger brother Ahmad (d. 1126/520).

After the Ghazzali brothers, sufism concentrated increasingly on *ma'rifah* as the only way to an authentic encounter with God. The experience and discussion of *hulul* became common, as did ideas of theophany. Teaching about *dhikr* (pious remembrance) became more and more sophisticated, and mystics interested themselves in musical seances, which Ghazzali had commended. 'Abd al-Qadir al-Jilani (1077-1166/470-561), a Persian who settled in Baghdad, studied both conservative Hanbali jurisprudence and *tasawwuf* and sought to resolve the apparent contradiction between them in his writings. He linked ascesis and ecstasy to a strict interpretation of *shari'ah* and attracted a large following. Even before his death he was widely venerated for his piety. Jilani and his contemporary Ahmad al-Rifa'i (d. 1183/578) were the first to organize their disciples into orders (*turuq*; sing. *tariqah*). Rifa'i preached poverty and patience to his adepts.

Shihab al-Din Yahya al-Suhrawardi (1155-1191/549-587), the first great Ishraqi, was born in northwestern Iran and lived in Anatolia for several years before moving to Syria, where he was arrested for blasphemy and presumably executed at the behest of Salah al-Din al-Ayyubi (Saladin). Suhrawardi expounded a sort of Aristotelian mysticism with many references to Hallaj and to Zoroastrian mythology. There is one wisdom and one mystical tradition, which is consistent with the Qur'an. Illumination emanates continuously from its absolute source, and those persons who have purified themselves and followed the mystic path ascend ever nearer to God until they experience *fana'*. There are still practising Ishraqi mystics in Iran today.

In Spain, *tasawwuf* reached its apogee with the work of Muhyi al-Din Muhammad Ibn 'Arabi (1165-1240/560-638). He was familiar with the ideas of earlier mystics but his own primary thesis discerned three types of knowledge: rational, sensual and mystical. The last comes directly and solely from God, and whoever has it knows everything. God is free from all attributes and so cannot be analyzed, but people can meet him in *ma'rifah*. Those who would meet God must first travel towards him, then in him, without straying from the *shari'ah*, until they finally arrive in the ultimate experience of evanescence.

Jalal al-Din Rumi (1207-1273/604-672) was born in northern Afghanistan but lived most of his life in Anatolia. He followed many mystic teachers until one Shams-i Tabrizi initiated him into an exalted stage of divine passion (*'ishq*). This launched Rumi into a brilliant career as a poet. His masterpiece was the *Mathnawi*, a chain of over twenty thousand couplets, which is both an exegesis of the Qur'an and a commentary on public morals, in the context of the overriding importance of divine love and the urgent need to seek it.

Of interest as a synthesizer of earlier thought was 'Abd al-Karim al-Jili (1365-1428/767-832), a descendant of Jilani who lived in Yemen and India and wrote a book entitled *The Perfect Person*. Jili followed the traditional sufi themes influenced by the ideas of Ibn 'Arabi and Indian mysticism. Written in the form of a series of conversations with God interspersed with supporting references to Qur'an and *sunnah*, his book describes the perfect person as a microcosm of the historical order, reflecting the powers of God and nature. Being is one. God, the pure being, is distinguished from being mixed with non-being (creation). The various attributes of being occur in all nature but they are discernible only in humankind the microcosm.

The Absolute, diffused in nature, returns to itself through humanity and in the process becomes one with the perfect person, who must by this new nature act as mediator between God and humanity. A person attains this perfect state through three stages: (1) learning the mystery attached to the various names of God and becoming one with one of those names, in order to be able to answer the prayer of someone who invokes that name; (2) meeting the various attributes of God (life, power, will, etc.), becoming one with them and coming to share them (which no other being in creation can do); (3) becoming absolutely perfect, absorbed into the essence of God. Jili always maintained that the perfect person was Muhammad, chosen by God as intermediary between himself and humankind, but Christian mystics could easily adapt his entire scenario to their own understanding of salvation history.

Sufi branches and orders

Techniques of remembrance acquired increasing importance to Muslim mystics after the thirteenth/seventh century, and some seemed to give these mechanics more attention than the gifts of God which were the ultimate objective. Mysticism also became more and more monistic, following an apparently Neo-platonic path of seeking the One in the soul of the mystic. Many of the later sufis distinguished between God the Creator and God the Judge of creation, with a tendency to assume that the soul and God were united. Such a position offended the religious leaders, because it denied the essential transcendence of the God of the Qur'an.

Mystics of the classical era expounded a unity of witness (*wahdat al-shuhud*). God reveals himself in the heart of the mystic while remaining one and transcendent. The mystic's ego encounters God through love and is ultimately consumed in the unity of God. Later sufis preferred the idea of unity of existence (*wahdat al-wujud*). The contingent world is merely a reflection of the one divine existence, and the human spirit is a direct emanation from the uncreated essence. Empirically existing beings can therefore be expected to dissolve through evanescence into God. The basic idea of the unity of witness is God's coming to the sufi's heart, while in the unity of existence the mystic soul returns to its origin through absorption into the divine essence which alone abides forever.

By the eleventh/fifth century, Islamic theology had lost much of its capacity to comment on religion. Having forcefully affirmed the transcendence of God, theologians had difficulty claiming to know anything about him or even how to please him beyond the word of the Qur'an. Philosophers similarly referred to God as someone remote, the First Cause whom it was almost impossible to contact except through much study and thought. Besides, many philosophers were in awkward dissonance with apparent teachings of the Qur'an about creation, eternity and resurrection. On the other hand, the religious scholars (`ulama'`) of the Qur'an and *sunnah* were more and more preoccupied with the practical application of *shari`ah* in the here and now, asserting that people could please God by obeying the rules. Increasing numbers of `ulama'` came to identify their interests with those of the political authorities. They preached civil obedience and accepted judicial office.

Many Muslims sought a closer awareness of God than what was offered by the censorious formality of the `ulama'` or the intellectual austerity of the theologians and philosophers. By offering people the very communion with God which the `ulama'` postponed to the next world, mysticism answered a religious need among the people. Its social and political dimensions offered a pattern of life and organization apart from the officially imposed law and order — which so often proved lawless and chaotic under tyrannical rulers or inefficient bureaucracies.

The quest for religiously oriented life-styles led growing numbers of people to meet at the homes of famous mystics, and these gatherings eventually resulted in the formation of several sufi orders. At first there were two tendencies, which may be characterized as ecstatic rapture and reverent sobriety. A few centres of study had won notoriety as early as the second century AH, but an enduring network of organized convents developed only some three hundred years later. Ghazzali gave *tasawwuf* a measure of official condonation, and some rulers brushed aside the qualms of the `ulama'` and patronized local sufis known for their piety. By the thirteenth/seventh century the convent (*zawiyyah*) was the normal focus of the Islamic community, and even people who did not engage in sufi practices would recognize the local sufi as their religious leader and worship at the convent mosque.

This accommodation was possible because most sufis conformed to *shari`ah* but offered a religious supplement to its legal provisions. It became common for a sufi to list an apostolic chain of spiritual predecessors, which was passed on to further generations of disciples. Mystic orders developed in interaction with trade guilds, and along the same lines. Some orders won official favour and material wealth, becoming as much a part of the establishment as the `ulama'` whom they had displaced. Other orders remained ascetic and poor and so continued to attract adepts in search of true piety. Virtually every corner of Christendom has also had its religious orders and other groups of especially zealous folk, some giving themselves to work for the poor and oppressed, others withdrawing from the world for more meditative or ecstatic contemplation. Some of these associations have persisted in holy dedication for centuries; others have fallen prey to disinterest and disorganization or even corruption and fraud. Thus both communities have positive and negative experiences to share in a spirit of mutual encouragement.

In the central Islamic lands, especially Iraq, the most important order was the Suhrawardiyyah, named for Shihab al-Din `Umar al-Suhrawardi (1145-1235/539-632), a man of deep spirituality who won the support of the authorities. He gave his official mantle (*khirqah*) to several individuals with only a superficial interest in mystic practices, including a few poets and political dignitaries, but his order spread to all parts of the Islamic world. The Rifa`iyyah had followers in nearly every Islamic country as disciples of Ahmad al-Rifa`i from abroad carried his teachings home with them. Some branches of this order were noted for their dances and feasts; others emphasized the triumph of spirit over flesh by inserting iron rings into their hands, ears and necks, walking through fire or charming snakes. Although the Qadiriyyah bears the name of `Abd al-Qadir al-Jilani, its links with him are quite tenuous. He was a strict conservative of the Hanbali school, and many Qadiris have criticized *shari`ah* as rigid impiety. Indeed, Jilani does not seem to have been a keen sufi and the chain using his name appeared some two centuries after his death. Today there are Qadiri centres in most Muslim countries, and the order enjoys particular importance in the Sahel region along the southern rim of the Sahara.

Of the several orders developed in Egypt and North Africa, the most influential is the Shadhiliyyah, whose founder Abu al-Hasan `Ali al-Shadhili studied in Seville and Baghdad and taught in the Maghrib before settling at Alexandria. The Shadhilis have not demanded rigorous poverty or even worn distinctive clothing, but they have tried to live as examples of pious devotion with restrained rituals.

Iranian mystics carried more Shi'i influence into their practices than the western sufis. For example, the Safawis, who emerged as the ruling dynasty of Iran in the sixteenth/tenth century, were leaders of a Shi'i order of sufis. A Central Asian who studied in Egypt, Najm al-Din Kubrá (1145-1221/540-618) returned to teach in his native Khwarizm. His disciples founded several branches, each claiming him as their forerunner. The most important of his heirs was probably Alá al-Dawlah Simnani (1261-1336/651-736), who followed the *shari'ah* and remained loyal to the restrained doctrine of the unity of witness but nevertheless won fame for his ecstatic experience induced by pious remembrance.

The Mawlawiyyah claimed to follow Jalal al-Din Rumi, whose order spread from Konya soon after his death in 1273/672. Using the precepts and practices set out in Rumi's poetry, disciples became famous for their musical exercises as "whirling dervishes", but the order never spread beyond Turkey. The Naqshibandiyyah followed the Tajik Baha' al-Din Naqshibandi (1318-1389/717-791) and became the greatest order in Central Asia, India and Kurdistan. The Chishtiyyah, founded by the Persian sufi Mu'in al-Din Hasan Chishti (1142-1236/537-633), stressed pious remembrance, auditory experiences and ascetic practices, and played a major role in the spread of Islam in India. Other noteworthy sufi *turuq* include the Bektashis, who were prominent in the Ottoman Empire, and the Tijanis, who have been very influential in West Africa.

These orders have generally been organized on a master-disciple relationship with spiritual tutorials and a few common exercises. Each individual usually enjoyed considerable freedom to develop under the leader's guidance. As *tasawwuf* became an entrenched element in the establishment, it began to attract charlatans and became diluted by antinomianism and superstition. Few great minds after the eighteenth/twelfth century joined the orders. Like the jurists, the mystics dug themselves into a tradition of imitation. Often people believed that ritual without piety or even sound doctrine could help them to know God. Only on the frontiers of Islam, as in India or West Africa, did orders like the Chistiyyah or the Tijaniyyah show any real intellectual and mystical life.

* * *

In all facets of human effort to communicate with the Creator of the universe, there are parallels of varying intensity between the experiences of Muslims and Christians. We have seen in this chapter and the previous one that philosophical and mystical traditions in the two faith communities have attested to similar experiences and developed congruent cosmologies, while contacts have been frequent and profound, so that it is quite reasonable to speak of a common heritage in either philosophy or mysticism, and even in terms of the debate between adherents of their respective human approaches to the divine.

This observation applies as well to general theological discourse within the two faith groups, and fruitful dialogue about the phenomenon of revelation has pointed the way to a constructive appreciation of each other's scripture. Important differences remain, of course, and are likely to endure for generations to come, probably until the Day of Judgment. But we can learn more of each other and even about ourselves if we learn from each other, even on the questions we can never humanly resolve, like prophecy and incarnation. Growing numbers of veterans of interfaith encounter from either tradition affirm that their understanding of their own heritage has been enriched by a prayerful exchange in a spirit of mutual respect.

6. Angles of Divergence: The Understanding of Law

Mystics, philosophers and theologians from Christianity and Islam can rejoice in their encounters and accept their agreements and divergences without greatly influencing everyday relations between the communities. More sensitive contrasts arise in the social disciplines of law and politics. Where mistrust is stronger than goodwill, recrimination has led to alienation. Eliminating or limiting misunderstandings, so as to lay solid foundations for enduring harmony, requires a thorough familiarity with the concepts and practices which have framed the legal and political perspectives of our neighbours over centuries of accumulated custom. This chapter surveys these elements of the Islamic legacy.

Jurisprudence

When we speak of jurisprudence, we are really referring to the complex issue of how personal ethics is related to public morality and political government. The tendency in Christian countries to entrust religious leadership to different persons and institutions from secular authority doubtless originated in the early experience of the church as a persecuted out-group. While instances of close identification of interests and individuals eventually emerged, the received wisdom generally upheld the principle of separation as the best guarantee of the autonomy which each element needed for the proper exercise of its duties. The adoption of Roman and Teutonic codes across Christian Europe paved the way for the adaptation of customary law in other societies in which the church would later prosper.

The Muslim attitude to law, one of the most characteristic aspects of Islam, grows out of the precedents set in the primordial Islamic state founded by Muhammad himself at Medina. The duty to rule is joined with the obligation to foster righteousness and protect the faith. Islamic law sprang from the precepts of the Qur'an and the example of the prophet; whenever the practice of the community was taken into account, whether in the form of ancient custom or pious conformity, it was always regarded as a secondary expedient.

Perhaps in no other major religious group is law so intricately bound to ethics as in Islam. Theology has little practical influence on law, and orthodoxy has been less important than orthopraxis. Indeed, the concept of orthodoxy does not really exist in Arabic; the term *rashid* implies proper conduct, not correct doctrine. This linking of law to ethics is of ancient Semitic provenance: Hammurabi issued practical ordinances which were supposedly sent by the gods, and early Judaism expressed a similar reverence for divine law. By contrast, Christian canon law has always been distinct from secular law (and usually from ethics as well). In the Jewish tradition, law developed gradually, growing from the popular tradition, but Islamic law, at least in theory, began with Muhammad. Roman law and common law were distillations of human experience, and Christian emperors codified Roman law while secular lawyers participated in the evolution of the canon. With no such ready-made system to adopt, the community in Medina laid the foundations of its own legal structure.

The informal legal notions of the pre-Islamic Bedouin aimed at sustaining social balance rather than an abstract idea of justice. When disputes arose, an arbiter was named to negotiate a new *modus vivendi*. Oaths were taken to ensure the validity of evidence, and the cornerstones of arbitration were avoidance of bloodshed and friction, and payment for satisfaction. For example, there were scales of compensation for homicide according to the perceived intent of the perpetrator and the status of the deceased. An arbitrator (*hakim*) rendered an opinion on any case referred to him, and it was common for a priest to be chosen for this role of determining the truth. The *hakim* held securities in the form of property or hostages which would be forfeit if his judgment was not approved. The collective memory gathered significant verdicts into a *sunnah* or corpus of what would be generally endorsed.

Meanwhile, the Meccans had produced a commercial code. Marriage law was very loose; often consummation was the only "ceremony", although a payment was usually made to the bride's father before the union or as soon afterwards as he learned of it. Except in questions about salvation, Muhammad did not greatly change the received *sunnah*. The Qur'an's major concern is ethical, urging justice and mercy. It encourages restraint and arbitration and denounces bribery, gambling and usury. The practice of stoning adulterers is not mentioned in the Qur'an and does not seem to have been the custom in Muhammad's time, but the Qur'an did introduce important modifications to marital concerns by imposing a waiting period on divorce, requiring any dowry to be paid to the bride alone and including mothers, sisters and daughters in the apportionment of estates. The Qur'an also enjoins believers to help the needy, but justice remains a private matter, for the injured party is the one who must initiate legal proceedings.

Every prescription in the Qur'an has quasi-legal implications, but the tenor of most of them is either ethical or ritual. The Qur'an's command to "obey God and his messenger" is the basis for adopting the tenets of Islam as a new *sunnah* which supersedes all pre-Islamic custom. But the Qur'an is no more a legal treatise than it is a theological document. It provides the foundation for Islamic ethics regarding business, government and care for the weak, but it gives no system of enforcement or punishment: chastisement in the after-life is the principal form of retribution.

In fact, most "rules" in the Qur'an cover proper performance of the five pillars or refer to specific incidents susceptible to general application; for example, the flogging of fornicators (24:2) or persons who have falsely accused someone of unchastity (24:4). Most ethical injunctions are difficult to apply as legal maxims: it is simple enough to enforce a prohibition of blood-feud but how can anyone determine whether a man is treating his wives equally? Many problems which were not addressed by the Qur'an continued in the purview of the received *sunnah*, but there were other matters which seemed to be partially covered. How could a judge decide whether someone was paying enough alms, and how could an offender be punished? What should be done if someone defied the Qur'anic rules of inheritance? While Muhammad lived, no system was needed but the expanding Islamic state urgently required an appropriate set of laws.

Muhammad supplemented the Qur'an by interpreting some verses. For example, he awarded heirs their Qur'anic allotments but permitted up to one-third of an estate to be left to a specific individual; this eventually formed the basis for the complex institution of pious foundations (*awqaf* or *hubus*). During the first decades after the prophet's death, his successor or *khalifah* exercised legal and political authority, and the only real legal question was who should be *khalifah*. The first two *khalifahs*,

Abu Bakr and 'Umar, took advice from the companions, but it was the *khalifah* who rendered judgment, although others could serve as arbiters when they were chosen by the common consent of all the litigants.

The Umawi sovereigns followed precedent insofar as they adapted the pre-Islamic *sunnahs* of the various provinces to the Qur'an and developed the system of *dhimmah* or legal protection for non-Muslim subjects. Thus, market inspectors were named according to the Byzantine custom. The Umawis named some other officials like the treasurer and the chief of police to act as judges in civil disputes. Such judgeships gradually became distinct assignments, and the judges were called *qadis*. Some were instructors of religion and ethics, and all were expected to follow the directions of the political authorities, even though such orders were issued only rarely. Where the Qur'an was not explicit and no record existed of a germane precedent from the prophet, a *qadi* followed the *sunnah* of his own city, perhaps modifying it slightly according to his own reflection. Soon enough there was a broad range of disparities across the empire, but *qadis* everywhere enhanced the importance of their office, which passed from a legal secretariat to a magistracy filled by persons of acknowledged piety rather than cronies of the governors.

We noted earlier that Islamic theology had its origins in the problems posed by the misrule of the Umawis. Questions about the legitimacy of Umawi governance also prompted the formation of small discussion groups to consider the social and ethical implications of these problems. In time, these groups emerged as "schools" of law. After the Abbasi revolution, people looked to the nascent schools to produce an Islamic polity for the state. The schools became more active and practical, adapting their thinking about ritual and theory to points of immediate social interest.

Emphasis shifted from holiness to legality, but the sacred never completely lost its place. Religious *'ulama'* were named as *qadis*. Virtually every province and city had its "school", two of which attained general primacy: Medina, because it was the city of the prophet, and Kufah, the school nearest the new capital of Baghdad. Other significant schools were located at Damascus, Basrah and Mecca. In each school the basic method of jurisprudence was to measure the local *sunnah* beside the Qur'an and adapt the former to the latter as required. Prohibitions of gambling and usury were combined to justify disapproval of selling "futures" on grain crops. At Kufah, this was extended to a prohibition of speculation on any movable property. "Doctrines" like this were simply the consensus of the *'ulama'* in the respective schools, but gradually each school developed its own general attitude, which of course became its *sunnah*. In Medina and Kufah, the *'ulama'* agreed to submit their individual opinions to a new criterion of judgment: analogy (*qiyas*). For instance, the minimum dower was set at the same sum as the minimum value of goods to be stolen to require the amputation of a hand — the loss of a hand being deemed equivalent to the loss of virginity.

Once an idea or a judgment was accepted as part of a *sunnah* it was considered to be binding on the local school as a precedent. The various *sunnahs* were opposed by people wishing to derive every new decision from the Qur'an alone or at least from the *sunnah* of the prophet, and these strict constructionists launched the major wave of *hadith* circulation, pushing proponents of the *sunnahs* to justify their practices through *hadiths* which they had themselves discovered. The last quarter of the second century AH was the period of greatest rivalry between local consensus and the so-called prophetic *sunnah*. At this time, Malik ibn Anas (d. 796/180) compiled his *Muwatta'* as a guide to legal problems. Malik identified *hadiths* which supported his school's teachings on various questions, thus rooting the *sunnah* of Medina in what Malik understood to be the revived *sunnah* of the prophet. The *'ulama'* in Kufah adopted similar methods, using Qur'anic stipulations and aligning local practices with the reported behaviour of Muhammad, but the sources used in Kufah differed from those of Medina precisely on points where the customs of the two did not match.

Generally, Medina was closer to pre-Islamic tribal ways, while Kufah, which had been settled by people from many provinces, showed the influences of the supranational Muslim community. Medina and its *sunnah* were therefore more Arab and more male-dominant and egalitarian. Kufah set women and men on a more equal footing but absorbed a class-consciousness derived at least in part from ancient Persian ideas. On questions of collective duty, the unit of responsibility in Medina was the tribe or clan, in Kufah the neighbourhood. Kufah's *sunnah* was open to outside influences in a way that was unthinkable in Medina with its weighty legacy as the home of the prophet and an area of pre-Islamic habitation. For example, Roman law affected Kufah's prohibition of slaves' owning property, but Medina adopted the classical Arab practice permitting them to do so. Kufah freed wards from all supervision by their guardians at the age of 25, but Medina recognized such liberty only upon the death of the guardian.

The *khalifah* Mansur, who ruled from 754-775/136-158, refused to impose any conformity in legal tradition. The Abbasis stressed the role of the *khalifah* as servant rather than master of the holy law; therefore, each school was free to evolve according to its own consensus through personal opinion or rigid application of the appropriate *hadiths*. Fearing irreparable damage to the unity of Islam, some people looked for a qualified expert to save the *shari'ah* from chaos by determining a sound basis for overall conformity. This was provided by Muhammad al-Shafi'i (d. 204/820). Having studied in all the major centres, he sought a synthesis of the schools which could serve as a universal *shari'ah*. Examining the various practices on diverse questions, he chose among them or tried to reconcile their points of view. Eventually he settled in Cairo to compile the distillation of his research during the last five years of his life. It is to this work that we owe the standard formula of four roots of jurisprudence: Qur'an, *sunnah*, consensus and analogy.

The Qur'an is of course the primordial source of God's revelation and therefore of God's will. The Qur'an also indicates how it may be interpreted or supplemented. For example, the injunction to obey God and his messenger shows that Muhammad is to be second in importance. Malik, arguing that Muhammad was not necessarily right all the time, had sometimes followed other precedents. The strict view insisted that Muhammad's reported words and deeds were the supreme exemplar for every Muslim. Shafi'i taught that Muhammad's legal precepts were divinely inspired and that the order to obey the messenger was equivalent to a command to submit to the book and the wisdom (Q 2:123), which he took to be Muhammad's divine inspiration.

The *sunnah* of the prophet is thus Shafi'i's second root. All the various schools claimed to derive their own *sunnah* from that of the prophet. Shafi'i inferred that it was urgent to establish a unified *sunnah*, so he attempted to do this through his own legal judgments. In practical terms, his interpretations of the Qur'an according to the *sunnah* made the *sunnah* more important than the simple wording of the Qur'an. His major problem, however, was the welter of contradictory *hadiths*. If conflicts could not be reconciled by explaining one *hadith* as reporting an exception to a general rule, Shafi'i tried to discern which had the better chain of transmitters or which reported a later incident, thus superseding an earlier episode. A *hadith* could abrogate other *hadiths* but none could overrule the sacred text, which they served only to explain. Nevertheless, the Qur'an did not supersede the *sunnah* because the *sunnah* exists to explain the Qur'an.

Shafi'i also adapted the idea of consensus (*ijma*') to his broad perspective. In his view a local consensus was no longer enough. Because the formula applied only to questions affecting every Muslim, any future consensus should embrace the entire Islamic *ummah*. Shafi'i accepted the *hadith* quoting Muhammad's promise that his community would never agree on an error, but he did not expect the *ummah* to achieve consensus on many issues. It is quite likely that his intention was simply to curb the influence of the several local concurrences. Finally, Shafi'i stipulated that any analogy must be demonstrably consistent with the Qur'an, the *sunnah* and the established general consensus.

In choosing these four bases for Islamic jurisprudence, Shafi'i rejected personal speculation and preference as too undisciplined and likely to cause too much diversity within the *ummah*. Although the four roots allowed some difference of opinion, this would be relatively uncommon and of scant practical significance. Shafi'i introduced nothing new to jurisprudence, and his contribution was in systematizing *fiqh* and eliminating the major sources of strife through a synthesis or reconciliation between the advocates of *hadiths* and the partisans of private opinion. Later jurisconsults (*fuqaha*') followed his four bases, even though there were variant emphases.

Nevertheless, Shafi'i did not achieve his goal of reconciliation. Some experts, eagerly adopting his attitudes, formed a new school of law, which was of course named after him. But most Malikis (followers of the school of Medina) and Hanafis (followers of the school of Kufah) adapted their own structures and adopted Shafi'i's bases while maintaining their own interpretations; and the major proponents of *hadiths* remained loyal to their position. Ahmad ibn Hanbal (d. 883/269) accepted only the Qur'an and the *sunnah*, thus originating the Hanbali school. By the late third century AH, however, Malikis, Hanafis and Shafi'is had reached a level of mutual respect and even Hanbalis acknowledged the pragmatic benefit of a measure of analogy.

These four schools have survived to the present day. The Maliki school, following the *sunnah* of Medina, is most important in North and West Africa, Sudan and Upper Egypt. Malikis adhere strictly to the precedents of their school and seldom refer specifically to *hadiths*. Hanafis continue the *sunnah* of Kufah and are thus nearer to the Shi'ah than other Sunnis. Hanafis have also been more rationalist than other *fuqaha'* and little interested in *hadiths*. They are now pre-eminent in Iraq, Turkey, South and Central Asia, and constitute an influential minority in the former Ottoman territories of North Africa. The Shafi'i proponents of "rational traditionalism" are now found mostly in Lower Egypt, East Africa, Indonesia and southern India. The stricter and more conservative Hanbalis are the principal school in Saudi Arabia, with noteworthy minorities in most other Islamic countries.

A system of five categories evolved for assessing human acts. Most actions are of indifferent quality, permissible but not praiseworthy; these are called "permitted" (*mubah*). Some actions are recommended (*mandub*): God rewards those who perform them but does not punish anyone for not doing so. Other acts are termed necessary (*wajib*), and God will punish anyone who neglects them. A fourth group includes reprehensible acts (*makruh*), which do not carry penalties but their avoidance is rewarded. Finally, there are prohibited actions (*haram*).

Most of the points of difference among the schools were of little consequence but some of the divergences have been more important. All agree that a man can simply repudiate any of his wives after he pays her dowry, but the schools differ on a woman's means of ending a marriage. Hanafis say that a woman may initiate divorce only if the husband is unable to consummate the union because of impotence. Malikis and Shafi'is allow some other considerations, such as impotence occurring after consummation, incurable disease of the husband endangering the wife's health, failure to provide for the wife's material needs, desertion, even cruelty. Other important distinctions involve inheritance and the custody of the children of a broken marriage. Generally, Malikis and Shafi'is are more interested in intent while Hanafis and Hanbalis base their judgments on external realities. The idea that the schools were four aspects of a single *shari'ah* eventually prevailed, with an appropriate *hadith* indicating that the prophet had considered divergence part of God's bounty.

From the fourth century AH, each school followed its own line, and *taqlid* (imitation) replaced *ijtihad* (personal effort). People limited their scholarship to commentaries on earlier works and originality narrowed to those points not yet settled by the school's consensus. For example, one essay warned against riding a camel which had drunk wine, noting the risk of contamination through the sweat of the camel but ignoring the more practical motives for avoiding such a mount.

Revival and reform

By the beginning of the fifth century AH, most Muslim theologians had fallen in line with Ash'ari's model, while the jurisconsults had adopted the principle of *taqlid* — imitating their predecessors. Little new was being thought in either of these disciplines. Meanwhile, Islamic philosophy had reached its apogee with Ibn Sina, and people like Hujwiri and Qushayri had won many to the sufi path. The Shi'i warlords of the Buwayhi family who held power in the central Islamic lands were unlikely to stem the drift towards sclerosis within the orthodox religious disciplines or to curb either the intellectualist aberrations among the philosophers or the spiritual escapism of most mystics. This decay eventually provoked some movements for reform, which in some ways resembled the many stirrings of new light or revival which have occasionally swept through various parts of the Christian world. No parallel is exact, of course, but renewal and return to pure values and teachings which have been somehow eroded or abused is a common theme among Christians as well as Muslims.

Fifty years later, political authority had passed to the Seljuks, a vigorous dynasty of Central Asian Turks linked to the Hanafi school of law and dedicated to reviving the *sunnah* and religious sciences. Although there had always been institutions of study in the Muslim world, the famous minister Nizam al-Mulk (d. 1092/485) introduced a new type of centre, called the *madrasah*, to train the legal scholars who would lead the revival. He built several, of which the most important were at Baghdad and Nisapur. The basic curriculum comprised *fiqh* (usually of the Hanafi school) and some inkling of *hadith*, philosophy, theology and exegesis, with occasional elements of mathematics and literature.

The most renowned teacher at the Baghdad *madrasah* was Abu Hamid Muhammad al-Ghazzali (1058-1111/450-505), who studied at Nisapur under Ash'ari and 'Abd al-Malik al-Juwaini before entering the service of Nizam al-Mulk. Nizam named Ghazzali professor in Baghdad in 1091/484; he taught theology and read philosophy there for four years until he had a nervous breakdown and went on pilgrimage. After a decade of ascetic practice in Syria and Khorasan, Ghazzali accepted a teaching position in Nisapur.

Ghazzali's writings underline the scope of his interests as a true "renaissance man". His refutation of the philosophers, written during his years in Baghdad, reflected disappointment with the philosophical approach to life and concluded with three arguments to show that philosophers were unbelievers. Philosophers said that the world was finite in space but eternal in time; Ghazzali contended that God created the world *ex nihilo* and could end or extend it at will. Moreover, philosophers limited God's role in creation to being the First Cause; Ghazzali asserted that God's continuing power allows him to act if and when he chooses. God existed before creation and could abolish it or alter it. Third, the philosophers asserted that only the soul is immortal, thus rejecting the idea of the resurrection of the human body which, they claimed, perished when the soul left it to be re-absorbed in the ultimate. Ghazzali insisted that the Qur'an promised resurrection and that God would not lie. His description of the giving of a resurrected body to every soul and his assertion of the unimportance of the material nature of this body offer a close parallel to Paul's teaching in 1 Corinthians 15.

Late in life, Ghazzali wrote a topical autobiography, notable for its explanation of his experiences as a sufi and affirmation that mystical meditation is more satisfying than theology or philosophy. He also wrote several theological treatises and a criticism of John's gospel. His *magnum opus* was a four-volume work on *The Revival of the Religious Sciences*, in which he discussed worship, social behaviour, the available encouragements for human hopes of entering Paradise and human virtues. As we noted earlier, Ghazzali killed rational philosophy in the Islamic East, but by reconciling sufism with theology he made mysticism respectable and helped it to become the principal form of Islamic religious expression for many generations. As well, he contributed to the development of *fiqh*, especially in a short catechetical essay on the *shahadah*.

Another sort of revivalism was the reassertion of conservative dependence on the Qur'an and *hadiths* typical of the Hanbali school of *fiqh*, which was always suspicious not only of philosophy, but also of theology and mysticism. During the Islamic world's political and psychological recovery from the Mongol conquest of Iran and Iraq, this stream of thought found a vibrant advocate in Taqi al-Din Ahmad Ibn Taymiyyah (1263-1328/661-728). Born into a family of *fuqaha'* who fled from Iraq before the Mongols and found refuge in Damascus, young Ahmad studied and taught *fiqh* and exegesis in his adopted home. He accepted various public offices, but he opposed innovations in the organization of the pilgrimage and criticized both *tasawwuf* and Ash'ari theology. He also expressed strong hostility to the *dhimmis*, the non-Muslim protégés of the state.

Persecuted by the establishment for his lack of conformity, Ibn Taymiyyah was eventually sent to Cairo in 1306/705, where he was incarcerated. Released after two years, he immediately resumed his attacks on the authorities, who quickly returned him to prison. Allowed to go back to Damascus in 1313/712, he spent seven months in jail in 1320/720 and six years later he was arrested for denouncing the veneration of saints. This time he died in custody. His views were often controversial, but he may have owed much of his trouble to his own violent temper and vehement personal abuse of his opponents. He was unhappy with innovative theology and monistic mysticism, but he was also worried about the drift of *taqlid* away from the basic teachings of the Qur'an and *hadiths*, which led him to argue for a reopening of *ijtihad* to allow people to make their own efforts to align their judgment and behaviour with "old-time religion".

Hanbalis remained a minority in most urban and agricultural areas of the Muslim world but this austere school won many adherents among the people of the oases in central Arabia. Several hundred years after Ibn Taymiyyah another revivalist appeared in Najd — Muhammad Ibn 'Abd al-Wahhab (1703-1792/1115-1206). Scion of a long line of Hanbali scholars, he studied in Medina and Basrah, returning to Medina in 1739/1152. After five years of indifferent success as a preacher in the city of the prophet, he formed a partnership with Muhammad Ibn Sa'ud, ruler of the oasis of Dar'iyyah, to extend the sway of "true" Islam.

This marked the birth of the Sa'udi kingdom, which gradually extended its realm over most of the Arabian peninsula under the political and military leadership of the prince's dynasty and the religious guidance of shaykhs from the Wahhabi clan. The Wahhabis prevented the incorporation of Najd into the Ottoman Empire, accusing the authorities in Istanbul of condoning and even committing serious abuses against Islam. At the same time, they subjected the Bedouin to unprecedented structural control, outlawing the veneration of saints and ending pilgrimages to holy tombs. As good Hanbalis, the Wahhabis allowed only the Qur'an and *hadiths* to be used as bases of legal judgments.

Other scholars during this period were also trying to revive interest in Ghazzali's work and in the notion of original Islam. In most cases, their motivation sprang from their discouragement with the empty rigidity of *taqlid* and a parallel dissatisfaction with the degenerate comportment of contemporary mystics. Another important factor was their growing awareness of the rising technical and cultural dominance of Western Europe during the centuries of complacent imitation in all branches of Islamic thought. The last Muslim kingdom in Iberia fell in 1492 and, after overextending their lines in Hungary, the Ottomans were in steady decline from 1571 on, although their retreat was slowed by jealousies among their rivals.

The first area of significant Muslim population to be governed effectively by a European power was the domain which the East India Company began to assemble in the late eighteenth century. Well before the arrival of the British, resistance to Portuguese encroachment had fostered a measure of revival among Indian Muslims. During his rule (1556-1605/963-1014) the Emperor Akbar tried to fuse Hinduism and Islam in a new religion called Din-i Ilahi, which hardly survived his own death. Akbar's innovations elicited a strong movement to restore orthodoxy, led by Ahmad Sirhindi (1564-1624/971-1034), which lasted until the end of the reign of the stoutly orthodox Emperor Awrangzib in 1707/1118. For several years, Muslim India had no leader until the rise to prominence of Shah Wali Allah al-Dihlawi (1702-1762/1113-1176), who was so intent on rallying the Muslims that he tried to issue legal judgments in conformity with every school of jurisprudence, indulging the preferences of various litigants. He and his sons personally translated the text of the Qur'an into Persian and Urdu to help their co-religionists understand its meaning.

Sayyid Ahmad Brelwi (1786-1831/1201-1246) eventually assumed leadership of the revival movement. He may well have visited the Wahhabis in Najd on his pilgrimage in 1823/1293; in any case, his followers resembled Wahhabis in their basic puritanism. In Bengal, Shari'at Allah (1764-1840/1178-1256) led a movement which resisted Hindu influence and British rule while attacking rich landowners of any faith. The `ulama' supported the Mutiny of 1857/1274, and after its defeat the "fundamentalist" torch passed to the Ahl-i Hadith movement and a stricter group called Ahl-i Qur'an, which rejected even *hadiths* as a basis of legal judgment.

On the opposite pole, Sir Sayyid Ahmad Khan (1817-1898/1232-1316) developed "modern" (i.e. Victorian) Islam, without miracles and with God as the First Cause of the philosophical tradition. In 1877/1295, Sir Sayyid founded the college which is now Aligarh Muslim University. Amir `Ali (1849-1928/1265-1348) and others described Islam as a quest for righteousness, while Muhammad Qasim Nanawtawi (1832-1880/1248-1297) founded the Dar al-`Ulum in Deoband to provide a centre for the study of *fiqh*, *hadiths*, exegesis and even theology and philosophy. This centre in Deoband accepted all four major schools of *fiqh* and issued judgments on many matters referred by Sunnis from every part of India.

This century's most famous Muslim modernist in India has been Muhammad Iqbal (1876-1938/1293-1357). Educated in Cambridge and Munich, Iqbal was a nationalist, a poet and an early advocate of a separate Muslim state in the northwestern corner of South Asia. He insisted that Europe owed its scientific knowledge to Islamic sources, but he adopted a rather Nietzschean approach to the interpretation of the Qur'an, with God as a superego. Nevertheless, he taught that worshippers are not detached from God but become perfect through love and prayer without an evanescent experience: pure worship is the most exalted state attainable in this world.

Abu al-Kalam Azad (1888-1958/1305-1378) was born in Mecca to an Indian married to an Arab, who had left India after the Mutiny. He moved to Calcutta at the age of ten. Azad disliked both the modernism of Aligarh and the sclerosis of *taqlid* and claimed to meet God in personal prayer through love; it was also through love that he had learned the *shari'ah*. Azad's original hopes for a new Islamic empire were frustrated by the emergence of Arab and Turkish nationalism, so he embraced Indian nationalism but not the notion of a separate Muslim state, and he remained in India after partition.

The religious leader on the other side of the Pakistan debate was Abu al-A'la al-Mawdudi (b. 1904/1322), who founded the Jama'at-i Islami in 1941/1360. According to Mawdudi, Islam is rational because it conforms to natural law, and Arabic is the best language for revelation. The *shari'ah* is binding for all time, and Muslims should be free to establish an Islamic state in order to obey the *shari'ah*. Mawdudi opposed the Muslim League's plans for a Western-style state for Muslims. He wanted Pakistani law to be an evolving *sunnah* based on the consensus of all qualified *'ulama'*. For the state to be truly Islamic, people would have to live in conformity with the model of the early Muslims. Only under a genuinely Islamic government could pious Muslims be free to practise their faith. Mawdudi was more religious reformer than political thinker, and his primary objective was the renewal of pure Islamic faith in South Asia.

The first great reform movement in Islamic Africa was launched by the disciples of Yahya ibn Ibrahim, a pious Berber chief, and his religious advisor Muhammad ibn Yasin. These two gathered a band of puritan warriors on a fortified island in the Senegal River. From this fortress (*ribat*) they took the name Almoravids (*al-Murabitun*). In the middle of the fifth century AH the Almoravids swept northwards, conquering North Africa and Islamic Spain. They built the city of Marrakech, which eventually gave the Spanish version of its name as the European label for the country of Morocco. The success of their military campaigns diluted the religious ardour of these warrior-saints, and soon a new wave of puritans rallied the faithful against the Almoravids' fatal combination of rigid *taqlid* and moral laxity.

The new rulers claimed to reassert the absolute unity of God and called themselves "unitarians" or *al-Muwahhidun*, but once again it is the Spanish derivative, Almohades, which gained currency in European languages. Muhammad ibn Tumart (d. 1130/524), who was their chief, assumed the title of *mahdi*, the one guided by God. But material comfort softened the theological zeal of the Almohads and their court became the home of several great Islamic philosophers. North Africa passed through a long period of strict Maliki *fiqh* and widespread popular mysticism, often attached to presumed descendants of the prophet, like the two families which have ruled Morocco since the demise of the Almohads.

This somnolent mixture of *taqlid* and veneration met its first strong critic in Ahmad ibn Idris (1760-1837/1173-1253), a sufi from Morocco who opposed the veneration of individuals and argued for a return to the Qur'an and the *sunnah*. Finding scant support, he moved to Egypt in 1799/1213, then some twenty years later to Mecca, but he finally settled in Wahhabi territory. One of his keenest disciples was Muhammad 'Uthman al-Mirghani, a Meccan who went to propagate Ibn Idris's reforms in Sudan, where his family continues a school of law and *tasawwuf* although it never regained the prestige it lost during its persecution under Muhammad Ahmad. The other eminent follower of Ibn Idris was an Algerian, Muhammad ibn 'Ali al-Sanusi (1789-1859/1203-1275), who spent many years with his master in Najd. After Ibn Idris died, Sanusi founded a monastery in eastern Libya, where he encountered much opposition because he rejected consensus and limited his judgments to the

Qur'an and *sunnah*. He also claimed to have unified all the sufi chains of succession in his own order. The puritan zeal of his adepts mobilized local resistance to Italian colonial rule and, although the Sanusis are no longer the royal family, Ibn Idris's ethic seems to motivate the current regime.

During the nineteenth/thirteenth century, a series of *jihads* in West Africa extended the area under Muslim government, won new converts to Islam and reinvigorated the piety of nominal Muslims. The most famous of these military campaigns, often conducted under the aegis of local sufis, was that led by Usuman dan Fodio, founder of the Sokoto state in 1804/1219. More renowned still is the movement of Muhammad Ahmad ibn Abdallah (1834-1885/1258-1302), a Sudanese sufi who came to believe that he was the *mahdi*. After some clandestine work, he publicly declared his call in 1881/1298. Within four years he controlled Sudan, but he died soon after his final victory over General Gordon. The Mahdist state survived another thirteen years until its conquest by the Anglo-Egyptian army under Kitchener. Muhammad Ahmad substituted his own *sunnah* for the four received schools and added to the *shahadah* a statement recognizing himself as *mahdi*. Preaching an egalitarian ideology, he expected to subdue the world in preparation for the Last Day.

Islamic revivalism was a major factor in resistance to French occupation in North Africa during the colonial era. This was especially true in Morocco, where the royal family became the focus of a programme to restore the religion of the first Muslims or *salaf*, which was only possible under an Islamic government. A final group worthy of mention is al-Ikhwan al-Muslimun, organized by Hasan al-Banna' (1906-1949/1324-1368), an Egyptian Hanbali who preached that Islamic culture could save itself only by returning to the Qur'an and the *sunnah*. From the founding of his society in 1928/1348 he created many embarrassments for the government and was eventually assassinated during the confusion following the Arab defeat in the 1948/1237 Palestinian war. Ikhwan remain an important force in Egyptian political life today, teaching that all Muslims are one family with one *shari'ah* based on the Qur'an and the *sunnah*, which provide all the constitution needed for the one *ummah*.

The spiritual antecedents of the Ikhwan's religious and political ideas are to be found in the pan-Islamic movement of the previous century. Three tendencies may be noted here. The first is a general sentiment that all Muslims are brothers (and sisters). Various Islamic peoples have developed along their own traditions but all sustain a vital interest in events affecting one another. Recent examples of this include the networks of concern for the people of Bosnia and Somalia in the wake of political and social upheaval and international vigilance over communal strife in India. Similar sentiments do not seem to extend to the predicament of the Kurds or the stand-off between Iraq and Kuwait.

A second form of pan-Islamism was the official Ottoman ideology for several hundred years. When Selim I conquered Egypt in 1517/923, he captured the puppet heir of the Abbasi *khalifahs* and apparently ended the caliphate. But in 1774/1188, in the Treaty of Kuchuk Kaynarca with Russia, the Ottomans declared that the sultan was the *khalifah* of the Muslims to balance the Russians' claim to protect the Orthodox Christians in Ottoman territory. Nothing more was heard of this claim until the reign of Abd al-Hamid II (1876-1909/1293-1327), who summoned Muslims everywhere to recognize his primacy. This appeal was rather late in the day and won only timid responses in countries which had already submitted to European rule.

Of more enduring significance was the pan-Islamic doctrine of Jamal al-Din, called al-Afghani (1839-1897/1255-1314). Probably born in Persia, he lived in Afghanistan and India and twice went to Mecca on *hajj*. Invited to lecture in Istanbul in 1870/1287, he drew a parallel between prophecy and philosophy and had to leave the Ottoman Empire in haste. He then settled in Cairo, where he received a government stipend and lectured on *fiqh* and theology for eight years, warning of the dangers of European encroachment and the need for all Muslims to unite in resistance. His ecumenical impulses were the positive conviction that Muslims should normally belong to one *ummah* and the negative belief that all the Islamic lands would fall under the yoke of infidel governments if the Muslims did not work together. Chased from Egypt, Jamal al-Din returned to India to oppose the work of Sir Sayyid Ahmad Khan, but soon moved to Paris, where he launched the journal *The Firmest Bond* and a secret society of the same name. This ardently pan-Islamic periodical did not survive but its influence long outlasted its short run.

Jamal al-Din was back in Persia in 1886/1303, invited by Shah Nasir al-Din. Soon they fell out, and Jamal al-Din travelled in Europe then returned to Persia but again disagreed with the shah. Invited by 'Abd al-Hamid, he then went to live in Istanbul. There was another falling-out, but the sultan kept the sage in honourable confinement. Implicated in an attempt on the life of Nasir al-Din in 1896/1313, Jamal al-Din died a few months afterwards. Fifty years later, his body was removed to a special mausoleum near Kabul. He had spent his life searching the world for the ideal Muslim ruler for the pan-Islamic movement; his best candidates and thus his biggest disappointments were Nasir al-Din and 'Abd al-Hamid, both of whom had their own hopes of enlisting his prestige for their private ends.

Jamal al-Din's greatest bugbear was the British Empire, and he strongly believed that both India and Egypt could have avoided occupation if Muslims had been devout and in solidarity. He had wanted to rally the *ummah* but he was so rationalistic that many accused him of trying to save Muslims from foreign rule through the destruction of Islam. Yet he seems to have been sincere in espousing the basic tenets of Islam in spite of the philosophical contradictions lurking in his own worldview. He advocated a return to the Qur'an and the ways of the *salaf*, who had been the original agents of Islamic splendour.

Jamal al-Din's leading disciple, the Egyptian Muhammad 'Abduh (1849-1905/1265-1323), was much more consistent and more moderate than his wandering teacher. Born in the Nile Delta, 'Abduh studied in Cairo, where he met Jamal al-Din during his first visit to Egypt. Suspected of mischief during the political troubles of 1882/1299, he joined his friend in Paris, returning to Egypt in 1888/1307, where he entered the judicial system. A decade later he was the mufti of Egypt.

Considering nationalism and open defiance of the British to be futile, 'Abduh sought to work with the occupying authorities in order to safeguard Islam. He supported the rejuvenation of Islamic education, especially to train Muslim youths to rebut the claims of Christian missionaries. 'Abduh hoped to modernize Islamic law by a process of *talfiq* or choosing the best rule on any question from among the four schools of *fiqh*. His adaptation of pious practices to modern circumstances were often so thorough that some wondered whether the result retained any essential elements of Islam. The followers of 'Abduh formed a number of distinct groups. A few seemed almost agnostic, but the most ardent of his admirers was the Lebanese conservative Rashid Ridá (1865-1935/1282-1354). He met 'Abduh in Lebanon in 1886/1303 and again eight years later, after which he remained his faithful disciple, moving in 1897/1314 to Cairo. At first, Ridá was pan-Islamic and pro-Ottoman but as his disappointment with Turkish nationalism grew he found new inspiration in the Wahhabis of Saudi Arabia. Islamic revival, in Ridá's view, should be based on the Qur'an and the *sunnah* only, and there should be no compromise with modernism. What is good in Western culture probably came from an Islamic origin, so Muslims should seek the Islamic sources for themselves.

In every part of the Islamic world today there are advocates of religious reform, and in many countries there are reformers of several tendencies. Almost everywhere, proponents of the ancient *sunnah* would allow only an absolute minimum of concessions to the changes in the physical and technological environment of a millennium. On the other hand, there are many who portray Islam as a modern faith consistent with every scientific advance and the ideal base for a pious life in a contemporary context, even if the ground rules may need a modest update. Each type of reform carries many social and political implications, but it is important to emphasize that the prime focus for every Muslim reformer is maintaining true religion and virtue. All Muslims have a duty to safeguard the right of their co-religionists to worship and live according to the precepts of the faith.

7. Angles of Divergence: The Understanding of Politics

In actual practice, the behaviour of devout Christians is quite similar to that of pious Muslims, motivated as both are by faith in God's mercy and a will to serve with gladness. But there is a fundamental difference between Islamic and Christian understandings of God's interaction with people which has important consequences in the area of religion and the role of government. Christians celebrate the resurrection of Jesus as a triumph over both sin and death, which is "the wages of sin". Only God is perfect, and by overcoming the inherent imperfection of human existence, Jesus is believed to have conquered death and paid the price of spiritual liberation and eternal life for all who would accept his mediation. Christians will continue to fall short of the grace of God and commit blameworthy acts in this earthly existence, and they will still take courage from their faith in Jesus' power to save them from the rightful consequences of their insufficiency.

Muslims agree that individual human beings cannot please God in an absolute fashion, but they see no need for an advocate or mediator to intervene between the Creator and a wayward creation. God has sent messengers to remind people that they will achieve happiness in this finite world and for eternity only through submission to the divine will (*islam*). Believers must seek their own spiritual well-being by observing prescribed rituals and, more importantly, adopting an appropriately sincere life-style, walking reverently "in the path of God".

Religion and public policy

The consequences of such a duality are obvious. Muslims expect their governments to oversee the observance of a whole range of religious prescriptions, from allocating suitable places of worship and collecting and distributing alms to maintaining a social environment in which the faithful may serenely comply with the requirements of piety. Civil magistrates must command good and prevent evil, and the best way of doing so (in the minds of Muslims everywhere) is to enforce the holy law passed down by successive generations of believers. Christians — and others — have espoused the view that faith is personal and have assigned the state the task of ensuring that all citizens are free to pray or not to pray according to their consciences. Under a secular constitution, Christians may work with like-minded members of other communities to influence public policy in the common interest. The question of fair treatment for minorities continues to pose a challenge to advocates of each of these systems in their various attempts to accommodate revered theories to the awkward realities of modern plural societies.

Shari'ah in its broadest cast is the way of righteousness, the path which the faithful should follow. Emanating from divine revelation, it represents the cumulative wisdom of wise and holy scholars who, through prayer and study, have developed specific applications for an elaborate array of life's circumstances. As these precepts are largely based on texts which have been taken to be the very word of God, it is extremely difficult for Muslims to accept any suggestion that their laws should be set on an equal footing with statutes of merely human provenance. Perhaps the best solution to the dilemma implicit in this situation lies in the discernment of regulations which conform to *shari'ah* and also meet the concerns of non-Muslim citizens.

Muslims are enjoined to live in peace with rulers who allow them to fulfil their duties, but they must make every possible effort to remove any impediment which an infidel authority might impose. On the other hand, it is the solemn obligation of a Muslim ruler to protect freedom of worship and any communal codes of subject populations. Contention has arisen only in modern times over such thorny issues as the suitability of a non-Muslim to lead in keeping with the essential guarantee to uphold religious injunctions and the fairness of giving all citizens the same treatment within a given country's legal and political systems.

The earliest genuinely political document in Islamic history, the constitution of Medina, was negotiated shortly after Muhammad moved there, although the text probably evolved during the time of the prophet's governance. Under this constitution, all the Muslims together formed a single *ummah*, distinct from other tribal groups, even those tribes from which the individuals had come. All loyalties and courtesies which had formerly depended on tribal bonds were transferred to the Muslim *ummah*. Muhammad was the arbiter of disputes because he was acknowledged to be the messenger of God and because he had been enlisted by the people of Yathrib to end their long civil war. After the Battle of Badr, Muhammad received half of all the booty, which made him much more powerful than any of his companions. This division of the spoils indicates that the prophet had gained recognition as the earthly leader of the *ummah*. His power continued to grow. During the last three years of his life, he was the autocrat, and the Islamic polity depended on his personality. People acted as his agents rather than as servants of the *ummah*.

The first *khalifahs* were similarly the focus of earthly power and authority. Their decisions were meant to be binding on all Muslims, although in principle they consulted the notables before issuing any decree. The foundation of the Islamic state was respect for the acknowledged successor of the prophet of God, and this remained the theoretical axiom through the Umawi and early Abbasi periods. As Abbasi power declined, the theory lost its practical substance. It was, however, during the eclipse of the Abbasis under a vigorous series of military sultans that the classical theory of Islamic governance received its definitive formulation.

'Ali al-Mawardi (d. 1058/450) wrote *The Principles of Government* probably in order to acquaint Abbasi princes with their true rights and responsibilities. There must be an *imam*, heir to political leadership of the *ummah*, and obedience to him is a duty imposed on the *ummah* by revelation, not reason. The *imam* is to be elected by the qualified representative or representatives of the community. Since it is possible to have only one representative, it was feasible for the sultan to elect, given that he had the force to impose his choice. The *imam* is to be a male descendant of the tribe of Quraysh, adult, brave, trained in law and physically and mentally capable of governing. A duly installed *imam* is responsible for the whole administration of the state, within the limits of the *shari'ah*. He may be removed only when he ceases to be capable of ruling — because of insanity, blindness, deafness, the loss of both hands or both feet, by falling into heresy or by losing his freedom of movement if the *ummah* is unable to obtain his release. An orthodox rebel can justify his action by winning and so becoming the new *imam* (this point covers the Abbasi revolution).

Subsequent religious theorists modified this classical model in the light of changing circumstances. For example, in a compendium written by Ghazzali for the governor of Khurasan, the imamate was said to be necessary for order in the world because the *ummah* alone cannot safeguard the religion revealed to Muhammad. The *imam*, says Ghazzali, deserves the absolute obedience of the *ummah*. This *imam* should defend the *shari'ah* and work to expand the area under the control of the *ummah*. Ghazzali followed Mawardi in seeing the sultan as the legitimate agent of the *imam* for keeping order in the *ummah* and confining the *imam* to religious functions — exemplary piety, legal erudition and the like. God will help the sultan in his choice in order to ensure stability in the *ummah*. Any rebellion is sinful because it defies God's election, but a successful rebel becomes the rightful ruler.

Writing after the fall of Baghdad at a time when the *khalifah* was obviously the prisoner of the Egyptian Mamluks, Ibn Taymiyyah had a radically different view of the Islamic state. He reasoned that God created the world to serve him and the state should therefore be subject to the *shari'ah*. The real unity of the *ummah* is not political but religious. The *imam* must govern according to the Qur'an and the *sunnah* on the advice of the *'ulama'*. Rulers are in fact mere agents of the revealed law and guardians of whatever the *'ulama'* declare to be law. Thus Ibn Taymiyyah would have transferred legislative authority to the religious scholars, as the Saudi government would eventually entrust legal formulation to the Wahhabi *shaykhs*.

Muslim philosophers derived many of their political ideas from classical Greece. Farabi said that politics is the study of human volitional behaviour with the objective of helping people to find true happiness. This goal is attainable only in the hereafter, but government should guide people to virtue as a preparation. Government is therefore the art of the philosopher-king, and good government entails certain practices to help people to virtue. These practices are learned through study and experience. The ideal state will endure as long as its succession of philosopher-kings avoids corruption and none deviates from the principles of government rooted in philosophy. Without philosophy, a state cannot become perfect, and an ignorant or imperfect state will never attain happiness or lead its people to virtue. Political science helps the ruler to lead individuals to those levels of happiness conditioned by their natural dispositions. An individual may hope to attain perfection only through political association with a state or nation under an ideal ruler. Each citizen finds happiness by obeying the ruler who is the heart of the body politic, both philosopher and prophet, who learns from God through rational communication (as a philosopher with active intellect) and through inspiration (as a prophet). States without virtue may be ignorant (seeking good where it is not), perverted (fallen from virtue) or evil (seeking such false knowledge or values as wealth, honour and sensual pleasure). In summary, Farabi tried to fuse a Shi'i doctrine of a pious succession of *imams* with the ideal state of Plato.

Although Ibn Sina wrote no specifically political treatise, his works refer to human happiness, which reaches its highest stage in the contemplation of God (Truth) and mystical union with the divine essence. Ibn Sina followed Farabi in linking Plato's philosopher-king with the Islamic *imam*, but his conception of a prophet is rather different. Whereas a philosopher must be taught such skills as logic, prophethood for Ibn Sina is a special endowment of the Holy Spirit, and a prophet is "normally" able to work miracles. Prophets are thus superior to philosophers, but they should improve their talents through philosophical learning. One can seek God only in a society whose people help one another to find the means of life. Such a community needs laws to govern relations among its citizens and a general law guaranteeing their spiritual integrity. This law is the *shari'ah* revealed to the prophet sent to teach people about God. Government must make people obey the *shari'ah* for their own happiness now and in the hereafter. Prophets give laws to the masses and show the elite how to serve God. In his ideal scheme, Ibn Sina divided society into three estates: sages, artisans and guardians. Each group has a president who names people to lead various subclasses. Individuals have allotted tasks, and the indolent must be destroyed (although unlike Plato Ibn Sina would not kill the infirm). Labourers are worthy of their hire and neither gambling nor usury is permitted. Guardians are paid from taxes, fines and booty.

Like Farabi, Ibn Sina portrays the ideal ruler in a synthesis of Plato and the Islamic *sunnah*: righteous, intelligent, brave, just and well-versed in *shari'ah*. The ruler should be elected by the *'ulama'* with the sanction of the general population. Usurpers and tyrants are to be deposed and executed, and a worthy insurgent opposing a bad ruler deserves public support. Persons violating the *sunnah* should lose their property and serve the faithful. The ideal state has a revealed law which it ought to introduce in any other state which it judges to be ready to benefit from such a reform. The state legislates for all its citizens in order to guarantee their welfare now and prepare them for the after-life; and only a few individuals can move beyond law to an intellectual union with God in pure gnosis.

More insistent than Ibn Sina on the *shari'ah* as an ideal revealed law, Ibn Rushd also regarded it as the constitution for an ideal state. This revealed truth is the same truth attained by philosophers through reason; philosophy is a companion and foster sister of *shari'ah*, but *shari'ah* is for everyone while only the elite can learn philosophy. Revealed truth is superior to reason because it comes directly from God, but only philosophers fully understand revealed law. This gives them the responsibility of safeguarding truth for the masses. Rulers should keep the public within the *shari'ah*, which properly administered gives everyone a chance to attain happiness. Ibn Rushd agreed with Farabi and Ibn Sina that politics, philosophy and prophecy have the same goal: gaining happiness for people by guiding them through a legal system. Plato's myth is an intellectual device, but revelation is superior because it comes from the Creator. *Shari'ah* is thus the basis for a perfect state. Wisdom, sound understanding and justice are the chief attributes of a good ruler, who should ensure that citizens learn basic beliefs. It is part of justice for individuals to know their own tasks and places. The ideal model was the constitution of the first Islamic polity as it was remembered by the *ummah*.

Farabi, the theoretician, adapted Plato's thought to an Islamic framework simply by identifying the philosopher-king with the *imam*, but made no comment on contemporary affairs. Ibn Rushd, the politician and courtier, tested the validity of Plato's ideas in contemporary events. In doing so, he often modified Farabi's teachings pragmatically, thus drawing nearer to Plato than Farabi had been. For example, both Plato and Ibn Rushd discussed oligarchy as a possible form of government, whereas Farabi merely put it into a notional list. Nevertheless, Ibn Rushd did not go beyond the synthesis of philosopher-king and *imam*, and his reflections confirmed the tendency of Islamic philosophers to offer the *shari`ah* as the ultimate good which would combine law and justice.

More pragmatic than most of the philosophers were the experienced administrators who wrote a genre of handbook called "mirrors for princes" intended to give instruction in the arts of governance. The principal counsel of the mirrors concerned methods for eliciting the best performance from subordinates. Like Machiavelli, they urged justice as being easier and less costly than oppression. Rulers should use their judgment in coordinating *shari`ah* with administrative regulation.

Like his Persian forebears, Jahiz (776-869/160-255) set the king's authority over the *shari`ah* and extolled compassion and justice as the most important qualities in a ruler. He named Muhammad the most excellent of human beings because he had promulgated the *shari`ah*, but then diminished the force of his own argument by noting that the *shari`ah* may well change with events. In any case, a prophet or *khalifah* must act as *imam* because the people cannot know their own welfare without divine guidance. Stated otherwise, divinely inspired apostleship fills the rationally stimulated sense of need for sound direction in the affairs of state.

One of the most powerful ministers in Seljuk Iran was Ghazzali's mentor Nizam al-Mulk (1018-1092/408-485), who held that the prime virtue of the state is stability, which is best ensured when the ruler is righteous. True religion leads to prosperity. The sultan rules by right of might and must be constantly on guard against potential usurpers. God decides who will rule, but it is prudent to help one's own cause. Victory and success are signs of God's favour, which can be sustained only through a network of spies to observe and control officials and to watch neighbouring states. To keep God happy, the ruler should encourage religion. The *khalifah* remains the symbol of Islam, but the real defender of the faith is the sultan who holds real power.

Nasir al-Din Tusi (d. 1274/672), who called himself a practical philosopher, was a Persian Shi'i in the service of the Mongol conqueror Hulagu. Tusi reasoned that people need a political association in a formal relationship with the Creator, as well as a currency to maintain equity. The *shari'ah*, mediated through the divinely inspired lawgiver Muhammad, provides this relationship, with Muhammad as *imam* and philosopher-king. The *ummah* needs a governor to control its affairs.

According to Muhammad Ibn al-Tiqtaqa, a descendant of the prophet's son-in-law 'Ali, the best state is the *khilafah*, even half a century after Baghdad had fallen to the infidel. However, current necessity obliged Muslim leaders to concern themselves with the contemporary kingdom (*mulk*). A just and moral ruler deserves the obedience of his subjects, and it is his duty to teach them morality. While the ideal ruler is a Muslim who instills the fear of God in his subjects, Ibn al-Tiqtaqa's criteria for rulership are pragmatic and reasonable: intelligence, justice, knowledge, the confidence of the subjects and firmness, especially in matters of defence. The ruler is responsible for the welfare of all his subjects but he should respect people with social status and influence in order to secure their support. The middle class can be manipulated with a combination of fear and interest, and the masses should be governed with awe, even fear if necessary. Ibn al-Tiqtaqa's bias is with the ruler, whose interests define the priorities of the state. A ruler is to be judged by his success in assuring the security and happiness (justice) of the citizens.

As a young man, 'Abd al-Rahman Ibn Khaldun held various positions in courts of North Africa and Granada, but he withdrew from political life around 1375/776 to live in a castle in western Algeria, where he spent four years drafting his *Introduction to History*. He left for the *hajj* in 1382/784, after which he became a popular lecturer at the Azhar University, in Cairo, where he taught for fourteen years, serving occasionally as the chief judge for the local adherents of the Maliki school. As well, he accompanied the army sent to defend Damascus but was obliged to help negotiate the city's surrender to Timur. He remained in Syria for a few months before returning to Cairo, where he was once again named *qadi* but died within weeks.

Claiming that the philosophers had lost touch with reality, Ibn Khaldun proposed a new science: the study of history. In his view, there are three types of society: nomadic, dynastic and urban. People need food, so nomads raid settled areas until a strong military ruler imposes order and establishes dynastic authority. The dynasty founds a city and a division of labour leads to prosperity, which eventually turns to luxury. The elite exploits the lower classes. Supposed needs increase, then taxes increase; people become poor and ill and the state cannot defend itself, so it collapses. A new nomadic dynasty sweeps from the desert and the cycle resumes.

Thus, Ibn Khaldun derives actual history from proximate causes, but the causal chain leads back to the First Cause, God. As creatures, we can never be familiar with God, but we can and should learn all we can about the rest of creation, and we should therefore study history and society. Good government includes the enforcement of the *shari'ah*. Natural and necessary because human life needs organization, the state is based on the power of the ruling group, and this power depends on the group's solidarity or *'asabiyyah*. When this solidarity decays, the state is supplanted by a new entity. To prolong the cycle, a ruler should act in ways that sustain solidarity and limit luxury, and the *shari'ah* offers the best balance between the rights of rulers and subjects. When a ruler usurps the authority of the *shari'ah* his government may become rational but it has already begun its decline, because a rational ruler acting in the interests of the dynasty will either oppress the subjects to the point of despair or indulge them to luxury. The *shari'ah* is therefore the best guarantee of political stability.

By re-infusing empiricism into philosophy and putting theology into this empirical framework, Ibn Khaldun produced the ultimate "mirror for princes". Thereafter, nobody in the Islamic world wrote much about politics for some four hundred years. The Ottoman Empire, Egypt and other states tried to modernize to counter the challenge of European imperialism but usually the proponents of reform argued for the revival of the true *shari'ah*, free from the accretions of centuries. There were some innovators, like Khayr al-Din Pasha, a Tunisian minister who drafted the modern Islamic world's first constitution in 1861/1278. This constitution leaves religion practically in the hands of the religious *'ulama'*; while it gives the *amir* the ultimate responsibility for protecting Islam; the religious courts control family and social law. Most Islamic governments effected such reforms late in the nineteenth/thirteenth century, at a time when several new conceptions of nationalism emerged to fill the void left by the failure of Jamal al-Din's pan-Islamism.

The Muslim nationalist Mustafa Kamil (d. 1908/1325) wished to base Egyptian society on Islamic principles but to provide for equal treatment for all Egyptians. He thus backed away from the narrow *shari`ah* which would give non-Muslims religious protection but subordinate status. Actually, the Ottoman Empire had enacted such a modification in its constitution of 1876/1293, but this document had been set aside by Sultan `Abd al-Hamid and was only restored when the secular, military Young Turks seized power in 1908/1325. `Abd al-Rahman al-Kawakibi (1854-1902/1270-1319), a Syrian critic of `Abd al-Hamid's oppressive rule, argued for an Islamic revival to be led by descendants of the first Muslims and a real *khalifah* chosen by the tribe of Quraysh. Although Arab Christians like Butrus al-Bustani had been singing the praises of the Arab nation for a generation, Kawakibi was the first Muslim Arab nationalist to make a public statement. His ideas seem to have distilled into the dictum that what is good for the Arabs is good for Islam.

These, then, are the most important influences on contemporary Islamic attitudes to relationships between religion and political life. Some have deep historical roots which have lost virtually none of their original force, while others have experienced some gentle modification through generations of application or slight adaptation in passing from one cultural region to another. The most obvious remark is that the Islamic world has known a variety of viewpoints and it should not surprise us today to observe a range of opinions on these questions across the world of Islam and even within any particular country. Muslims and Christians alike should resist any temptation to portray a monolithic mindset — for which there is substantiation neither in any current context nor in history.

Some specific features

Certain penal provisions of the *shari`ah* have acquired extensive notoriety. The stoning of adulterers is indeed canonical, but only on the testimony of four eyewitnesses, which would suggest that the offence would have to be of truly flagrant insouciance. The amputation of the hands of thieves is also a valid penalty, but those who steal because of financial distress are generally exempt. Occasionally, Muslim governments have outlawed the sale of alcoholic beverages, but such a prohibition would not normally apply to sacramental wine used by Christians or members of other subject populations; and in any case there are numerous instances of Christian administrations enforcing similar bans. Likewise, modest dress is almost universally required, although there is considerable cultural latitude in defining the parameters of the permissible.

Several aspects of Muslim family practice should be noted. Muslim men may marry women from a number of communities, including Christians, but Muslim women may marry only Muslims. Where Muslims are a religious minority (Europe and North America) or local pre-Islamic norms have survived (West Africa), there may be occasional exceptions to this rule, but most traditional Islamic societies have shown great severity in punishing transgressors. Muslim husbands are supposed to ensure that spouses from another faith-group have every facility for the untrammelled observance of their own spiritual requirements, but the children must be reared as Muslims. Here again, exceptions may be found, especially in religiously plural contexts where individuals feel free to choose their own affiliation rather than bound to follow an established order.

Islam has no concept of sacraments, and marriage is seen as a simple contract between the spouses. A husband must provide certain guarantees for the well-being of each wife, but divorce is relatively quick and easy, with the major provisos ensuring the proper ascription of paternity for any child born after a separation. Small children remain with their mothers, but at a given age (usually around seven years) they rejoin their fathers. Christian women who marry Muslim husbands are generally aware of these regulations, but misunderstandings over custody have been common. In some areas, there have also been cases of Christian widows and their offspring being denied an equal inheritance with their Muslim co-wives and half-siblings. The ongoing debate about how to apply the Qur'anic stipulation that all wives should be fairly treated goes far beyond the confines of interfaith debate, and we may conclude with the observation that the Christian ideal of a sacramental, lifelong monogamous union and the Islamic model of pragmatic, egalitarian polygamy offer a notional contrast which each side has blurred by a cloud of nuances.

As several Islamic states have attained impressive new economic muscle in recent years, Islamic banking theories have attracted much attention. Most Christians are familiar with the theoretical and theological distinction between usury and interest; for them, exorbitance is sinful but a fair return on investment is quite legitimate. *Shari'ah* has been stricter, taking the Qur'anic prohibition of *riba'* to cover all types of accrual based on preset rates. Islamic banks have provided other forms of managing wealth which do not offend the received interpretation, such as sharecropping or joint risk-taking. Critics have expressed earnest scepticism about the viability of such enterprises, and many Muslims have preferred to adopt a reading of the proscription which equates *riba'* to usury and allows them the same options as their partners or competitors from other backgrounds. Financial institutions will doubtless persevere in developing an elaborate series of hypotheses for testing by the double ordeal of markets and magistracies.

Where public education has been available, Muslim parents have tended to prefer sexually segregated systems, although in Canada and elsewhere Muslim teachers and students have long participated in co-educational programmes. Along with respect for appropriate standards of decorum, they have insisted on retaining within the curriculum some provision for the inculcation of moral values. They have not been alone in this advocacy of course, and many strong interfaith alliances in local neighbourhoods have originated in common promotion of family solidarity and shared opposition to the spread of pornography or excessive violence in bookshops, cinemas, popular music or video-cassettes. Beyond such expedients, plural societies in many lands have demonstrated a growing willingness to use their schools to nurture an informed and respectful awareness of the basic tenets and characteristics of the various faith communities within their borders.

Justice, peace and the integrity of creation constitute a triad of interrelated causes to which the 1983 assembly of the World Council of Churches committed the ecumenical movement over the closing decades of the twentieth century. Each of these concepts has always held a prime position in Islamic doctrine, and an affirmation of their mutual dependence would surprise Muslims only if it was put forth as a novelty. The tight weave between law and theology through long centuries of Islamic history underlines the central place which justice has enjoyed in the elaboration of political and social theories derived from exegesis of the Qur'an. Furthermore, the same holy book assigns to humankind the awesome privileges and responsibilities of being God's own vice-gerents on earth; one could hardly hope to find a closer parallel to the WCC's theme than this depiction of our human duty to every other creature. And peace, a deep and comprehensive sense of being in harmony with the Creator and all creation, is constantly on the lips of every Muslim, invoking this most abundant of blessings on each person encountered along the pathway of life.

Generosity and hospitality are everywhere esteemed, and Muslims are as active as anyone in providing for widows and orphans, caring for invalids and the elderly and sheltering refugees. Pious foundations (*awqaf* or *hubus*) have operated a rich variety of hospices, clinics and similar establishments in all parts of the Islamic world and in every age. During the centuries of Christian Europe's persecution of the Jews, Muslim governments from Spain and Morocco to the Ottoman Empire and Iran regularly gave asylum to refugees from any sort of maltreatment or fear, and allowed their religious minorities broad autonomy in running their internal affairs. The contrast with medieval Europe and the Inquisition is very positive in terms of Islamic principles of fairness and respect for human rights, which could be of great inspiration to modern leaders as they seek to assure the same objectivity in today's changing circumstances.

* * *

Muslims and Christians have much in common. They worship the one God, who has revealed the divine will to humankind and continues to watch over the bountiful world which has been ours to use and abuse since the beginning of time. They sense a responsibility to their Maker for their stewardship of creation and of the talents and assets allotted to them as societies or individuals, while the philosophical and mystical legacies which enliven their intellectual and spiritual discourse have drawn from generations of intensive exchange. They hold similar social and family values; and their attitudes to public issues, formulated in a variety of contexts, build on congruent conceptions of justice and equity. It is tempting at times to stress their theological or ethical differences and despair of finding any grounds for meeting or any way to go forward together. But it is equally possible to develop the points of contact and transform the divergences in such a manner that each community may sincerely praise the Lord of the universe for their concurrent enterprise and mutual witness.

8. Modes of Relationship

Well before the Prophet Muhammad and his companions settled in the oasis of Medina and founded the first Islamic state, they had had several sorts of relationship with the Christians of Arabia and nearby countries. Some of their earliest impressions were frankly negative, especially regarding the key doctrines of the Trinity and the Incarnation, which so manifestly contradicted the Qur'an's affirmation of God's unique essence and absolute otherness. Although they were impressed by the piety of many Christians, including the monks of Sinai, the Muslims could not endorse the austere and celibate life-style practised by the hermits, and the dictum of "no monkery in Islam" has survived through the ages. Even the most ascetic Muslim mystics have been married, and no monastic movement has ever appeared in the Islamic world. Furthermore, Islam has had neither ordained priesthood nor special hierarchy, but has simply assigned leadership to persons of recognized piety and scholarship (though among the sufis spiritual authority has normally been transmitted by chains of sponsors or *pirs*). At the same time, there were very positive appraisals of the role of the Christian king of Ethiopia in giving asylum to the many Muslims forced to flee the persecution of the Meccan aristocrats, as well as sympathetic accounts of the encouragement which Christians had offered Muhammad in the early years of his apostolate.

The Qur'an evokes a similar range of options for interaction with Christians. Several passages scold them for altering revelation or scorning Muhammad's claims and incite the Muslims to struggle against them in the cause of the true faith. Many sections decry the spiritual obduracy of the Christians who insist on their own dogmas, while other passages seem to suggest an attitude of reciprocal accommodation. A few verses are even more conciliatory, urging friendship and cooperation. As it would be inconsistent to follow all these indications simultaneously, Muslims have taken them to refer to dissimilar situations and applied them with varying force to the great miscellany of circumstances in which their encounters with Christians have taken place.

Christian ideas of divine economy and social order had gradually assumed a certain aura of permanence during the centuries preceding the advent of Muhammad. His message posed a serious challenge to the doctrinal and political formulas which secular and ecclesiastical authorities had begun to elaborate at the time of the Constantinian revolution of the early fourth century. However, the first Christian responses to the new teachings were generally more political than religious, and often they reflected more concern about rivalries among Christians than any specific opinion about Islam.

Politics and doctrine intersected at the very beginning of Christian-Muslim contact. Byzantine emperors and their disaffected subjects had so irrevocably fused political loyalty to religious orthodoxy that any doctrinal disagreement entailed not only heresy but also treason. The entry of the Muslims into the fray simply added one more element to the confusion. Ever since, Christian attitudes to relationships with Muslims have depended on a cluster of missiological orientations — ranging from triumphalism to relativism — and on the particular social and political dynamics prevailing in each context. From patronizing indulgence of a distracting annoyance to paranoid anxiety about the agents of the apocalypse, Christian polemics through the ages have better reflected fluctuations in the church's self-confidence than the status of any theological debate or military confrontation. Occasionally, free spirits have sought new directions, and every generation has had its advocates of a more open and trusting exchange.

This chapter will survey six different patterns according to which Christians and Muslims have articulated their involuntary symbiosis over fourteen centuries of uneasy experiment.

Confrontation and conflict

> Who is more unjust than one who forbids that God's name should be mentioned in places of worship and tries hard to destroy them? (Q 2:114).

> Fight against those who have been given scriptures but do not believe in God or the last day and do not forbid what God and his Messenger have forbidden and do not practise the religion of Truth, until they pay tribute willingly and are humble (Q 9:29).

During his decade in Medina, Muhammad formed alliances with most of the tribes of Arabia. Abu Bakr's first task as the prophet's *khalifah* or successor at the head of the Islamic state was the reassertion of the Muslims' authority over the whole peninsula. Significantly, the real object of this campaign was understood to be the extirpation of apostasy rather than the suppression of separatist rebellion. When Muslim armies occupied the Fertile Crescent, Egypt and North Africa, their leaders negotiated treaties with local authorities (often bishops), guaranteeing freedom of worship to the subject populations. Those communities which resisted and eventually succumbed would have to shoulder a much heavier tax burden than their more compliant neighbours. Otherwise, life varied little, and over the next few centuries some territories changed hands frequently with only annoying inconvenience for the inhabitants, whatever their religion.

The arrival of the Crusaders in the eastern Mediterranean brought intolerance and bigotry to new depths, notably with the Frankish army's massacre of the Jews and Muslims of Jerusalem in 1099. War became an act of misdirected piety, with zealots in every camp armed to uphold their own beliefs by force and pillage. The stated object of the Crusades was the restoration of the holy places in Jerusalem to Christian rule, but mass murder and double-dealing quickly sapped the expedition of both legitimacy and credibility. Several verses of the Qur'an, like the first one quoted above, were invoked to urge Muslims to active combat against anyone who would prevent Muslims from fulfilling their ritual obligations. The idea of *jihad*, which had originally involved a personal effort to enhance one's spirituality, acquired a new thrust as a communal commitment to protect the territory and prerogatives of the Muslims, and even to extend the domain of the Islamic *ummah* whenever and wherever possible.

Along the fringes of the Seljuk sultanate in Anatolia, warrior-knights raided, assembling a string of small states which gradually merged under the Osmanli dynasty to become the conquerors of Byzantium and the masters of the Balkans. A parallel process in the opposite direction marked the inexorable consolidation of the Spanish kingdom and its eventual absorption of all Iberia. The cavalier tradition moved to a grander stage in the sixteenth century when Charles V and Süleiman the Magnificent wrestled for control of the Mediterranean and military supremacy in Europe. Religion was certainly not the only impulse driving the war machines, but economic and territorial factors were much easier to justify when the enemy was an infidel, and both sides were doubtless sincere in claiming their God was with them.

Warfare continued to be the primary pattern of interaction between Muslims and Christians throughout the era of European economic expansion and the colonial occupation of many Islamic countries. Muslims who linked prosperity with righteousness often attributed their military and economic misfortunes to moral laxity, rallying opposition against the imperialists with calls for a return to the pure fundamentals of divine religion. Rulers who seemed to have compromised their faith in order to keep office were the objects of the most vehement derision, and waves of puritanism swept renewal movements to power across the African savanna and southern Asia. Meanwhile, authorities in the Ottoman Empire and elsewhere introduced a variety of reforms designed to adapt their societies to the modern world without diminishing the essential elements of Islamic faith and order. The verdict of events proved ambiguous: the Europeans overran the statelets of India and the Sahel, and the only major entities to escape subjugation were the austere kingdom of the Sa'udis in the Arabian heartland, the eagerly reformist Turkish republic and the firmly traditionalist monarchy in Iran.

Whether the obstacles were administrative regulations or military fiats, resistance was fiercest where alien officials impeded the observance of religious duties. At first, rebellions were few and futile, like the campaigns of 'Abd al-Qadir in Algeria or the rising in Somalia of the Salihiyyah under mullah Muhammad b. 'Abd Allah. The Muslims' abiding conviction of the rightness of their cause sustained a persistent effort to expel the interlopers, although many leaders opted to use the system in place to achieve the same objectives. Eventually, another Algerian insurrection would succeed, and by one means or another Islamic peoples from Morocco to Indonesia gained their independence. Christians in these lands had generally supported the national movements, but in certain areas hostility lingered, fuelled by the suspicion that they had somehow been the allies or the favourites of their co-religionists from abroad.

Today, there are still intransigent and vocal defenders of such measures as the taking of hostages, the bombing of public institutions and the waging of outright war against the presumed enemies of Islam. Some are triumphalists, desiring to impose their version of *shari`ah* — usually narrow and rigorous — wherever Muslims constitute a majority. Some, inspired by another age, would use force or guile to expand the area under Muslim rule in the hope of proving the moral and practical superiority of Islamic governance and redressing the perceived inequities of recent history. Another group draws its partisans from visionaries in countries where Muslims feel somehow beleaguered, driven to spectacular acts of violence in the service of Islam and social justice.

Certain Christians portray these extremists as the norm and echo the call for vigilant confrontation as stridently as any of their adversaries. They can find nothing good in the *shari`ah*, for they too adopt the sternest readings, intending thereby to warn the churches and other communities of the sorry fate awaiting any who would collaborate with Muslim compatriots. Even journalists and politicians who do not consider themselves very religious often become willing accomplices of these hard-liners by oversimplifying situations without explaining them and implanting in the minds of their readers and hearers unfair caricatures of either faith and its adherents. Finally, there are parts of Lebanon and some other countries where religion has been swallowed by a monstrous vortex of undistilled enmity that threatens to devour every vestige of human feeling in a paroxysm of spite, to the desperate shame of both communities of belief.

Agreement and alliance

> And if they incline to peace, incline yourself to it as well, and trust in God, for he is the all-hearing, all-knowing (Q 8:61).

> Excepting those of the idolaters with whom you made a covenant and who have not subsequently failed you in any way, nor helped anyone against you — with these fulfil their covenant until their term; for God loves the pious (Q 9:4).

Although Muhammad contracted accords with tribal chiefs from all Arabia, the Qur'an denounces most of these partners as perfidious turncoats fit only for the most painful chastisement. To be sure, some kept their word, thereby earning the Muslims' respect and goodwill, at least for the duration of any given agreement. Such compacts were tactical understandings, but breaking them was breaking faith — with the Muslims and implicitly with God. Their religious import became evident when Abu Bakr used the very first rebellion to justify his proscription of paganism in every quarter of Arabia. The conquerors of the provinces beside the Mediterranean signed a series of unequal arrangements with local authorities, but eventually emissaries from the supreme command negotiated formal treaties to fix the imperial frontiers in Anatolia and Iberia.

For several centuries, a cycle of skirmishes and parleys determined the fluctuations of the boundaries of the Byzantine Empire and the caliphates, setting changing limits for the petty states of either persuasion bunched along the line of scrimmage. Princes on either side forged alliances according to their own political interests, and a common chivalry infused the continuing interplay. In time, even the Crusaders who served in the Latin enclaves learned the rules of the game, and the legends about Salah al-Din and Richard Cœur-de-Lion are as much popular reflections of this cultural assimilation as they are accurate biography. Peasants and townsfolk were free to continue in their own faith, untouched by the transient tides of government except for the occasional redesignation of a particular building as a church or a mosque.

Over time an atmosphere developed which allowed Muslims to accept Christian governors as long as these rulers made proper provision for the exercise of religious obligation. The Spanish Inquisition and the forcing of all Iberians into Christian baptism contrasted sharply with the official toleration practised by Islamic states from the Ottoman Empire to the smallest emirate. The principle survived in Islamic jurisprudence to encourage the so-called modernists in India, Indonesia, Egypt and North Africa to work with relatively benevolent colonial officers on behalf of their fellow-Muslims caught in the dilemma of infidel suzerainty. Indirect rule proved a convenient buffer for astute European functionaries and their local partners alike, since it perpetuated a semblance of Islamic authority while facilitating the integration of the desired territories into the overall imperial design. The retention of vast tracts in

subjection soon became strategically unnecessary and economically untenable, and protectorates like Morocco and Tunisia
regained their independence with considerably less acrimony
than Algeria, which had experienced the dubious privilege of
incorporation into France.

From Mauritania and Senegambia to Sulawesi and Mindanao, Muslim populations were militarily and economically
at the mercy of the European and North American invaders.
The newcomers could choose brutal repression or benign
restriction; they could even try to ignore the importance of
religious sentiment entirely. They often governed capriciously, but in those cases where the system of indirect rule
was applied with some consistency, it eased the trauma of
massive foreign interference in local affairs. In classical
terms, the state of alliance (*mu'ahadah*) could pertain only in
areas ruled by non-Muslims. Whether the Muslim population
formed a majority of the inhabitants was not of immediate
concern, as long as the Muslim component of the local
society could muster sufficient economic or social influence
to merit the attention of the governors. In the variety of
circumstances found in colonial Asia and Africa, each
specific context produced an indirect administration adapted
to serve the military and commercial interests of the foreign
occupiers and to preserve the dynastic legitimacy of the
indigenous leadership.

The relative success of any experiment depended considerably on the ability of the leaders to articulate the religious
aspirations of their subjects and to assure the free practice of
worship. In Kashmir, Hindu princes and British residents
retained the watchful indulgence of a largely Muslim
populace, while British officers in the Deccan worked with
the Muslim *nizams* to govern a heterogeneous community in
which Hindus constituted the most numerous single element.
In places like Sokoto, the British presence actually helped the
consolidation of Islamic consciousness, both by rallying the
determination of the local Muslims and by restricting the
activities of Christian missions in the interests of political
calm.

To escape persecution at the hands of the Meccan aristocrats, some of the very first Muslims had sought refuge on the

western shores of the Red Sea, where the *negus* of Ethiopia had assured their safety. His gesture began a long history of positive contact between this Christian kingdom and its Islamic neighbours, while successive dynasties continued the tradition of toleration for their Muslim subjects. The Ethiopians defended their independence throughout the era of colonial expansion, succumbing only to Mussolini's armies for a brief five years. Their perseverance encouraged Muslims and Christians all over Africa to work for social and political harmony free from foreign interference. In the closing years of Haile Selassie's reign and under the revolutionary regime which followed, ethnic and religious suspicions ironically caused this noble heritage to deteriorate to the point of armed confrontation. But we can hope with some confidence that immediate interests and shared memories will combine to revive the friendly habits of a millennium.

A similar record of tranquillity developed in Meroe, between Ethiopia and Egypt. Eventually, this Christian monarchy weakened and disappeared, and most of the populace converted to Islam. Late in the nineteenth century, this area was the theatre of operations for Muhammad Ahmad al-Mahdi, the leader of a movement to purify and fortify the Islamic presence. The *mahdi* expelled the European representatives of the Ottoman government, who bore a double stigma as aliens and infidels, but a few years later his successors surrendered to Lord Kitchener. The "Anglo-Egyptian Sudan" became the local model of indirect rule. This self-styled condominium extended its authority southwards up the Nile, permitting a number of Christian missions to work among the local communities. As a result, Sudan emerged from colonial rule in 1956 with a highly complex political and social structure. The rival Muslim groups vying for supreme power adopted generally ambivalent attitudes to the mostly Christian southerners. For their part, the southern peoples pointed to their ethnic, linguistic and religious differences from the northern, Arab Muslims, and sought to negotiate a balance which would allow them sufficient autonomy to safeguard the survival of their own institutions. A generation of independent statehood has brought a series of experiments without producing a durable solution.

Protection and propriety

> How can it be that when they have the advantage over you they respect none of their engagements to you, whether for kinship or honour? (Q 9:8).

> You will be called against a formidable people, to fight against them until they surrender (Q 48:16).

Muslims have a solemn duty to protect all who would worship the one God and to intervene against any ruler who prevents Muslims from observing their own pious obligations. From its earliest days, the first Islamic state had to be wary of the propensity to treachery and inconstancy current among the nomadic tribes of Arabia. Where treaties were kept, there was no need to fight, but it was most important to show that oppression or betrayal would be immediately and severely punished. As the Muslims extended their dominions, they subdued any state which had proved unreliable, exacting a head tax (*jizyah*) from their new subjects. They had no mandate to spread their religion by the sword, but they did claim the right to make each territory safe for the free practice of Islam. In exchange for paying the head tax, the conquered peoples received the protection (*dhimmah*) of the Muslim government, which allowed them to follow every aspect of their faith, but relegated them to a status of economic and political inferiority.

The second verse cited above reflects the standard rationale for vanquishing the opponents of Islam. The Qur'an, however, uses the word *dhimmah* only twice (9:8,10), to refer to a pact of honour. Some forms of this root evoke rights and security, but others carry meanings of blame and shame. The ambiguity inherent in the etymology has had more than academic significance, for there has been a general and persistent tendency in popular attitudes to castigate non-Muslim "protégés" for their obduracy and to interpret any discrimination which they might suffer to be a consequence of their spiritual shortcomings and evidence of divine disapproval.

In the Mediterranean provinces from Syria to Iberia where Muslim governments initially held sway over large numbers of Christians, security of property and freedom of religion were welcome innovations after long years of internecine feuding among the various ecclesiastical factions. The schisms and sects of the church were of little interest to the Muslims, who sought only to impose and preserve order, and the loss of military strength robbed the Christians of the means of fighting among themselves. Conversely, Christians had little to do with the doctrinal and ideological nuances which fed the major internal disagreements within the Islamic leadership, so the passing of successive Sunni or Shi'i dynasties had scant impact on the subservient autonomy of the local church.

The idea that all the subjects of a Christian monarch should espouse a common version of the one faith gained wide currency after Constantine transformed the church from a persecuted martyr community into an official and powerful religious establishment. Political and social incentives induced most pagans to accept baptism, but a few Jews were more or less tolerated as merchants and bankers. Their social position was always subservient and their persons and fortunes were constantly vulnerable to the whims of Christian rulers, who had an armoury of pretexts for any imaginable torment or confiscation. When the vagaries of warfare brought Muslims in Syria, Spain and Sicily into the ambit of Christian polities, they were forced to share the same sorry lot as the Jews, heretics and schismatics already on the scene.

In Muslim countries, then, other "people of the Book" (including Christians) had a second-class standing that nevertheless generally assured them the freedom to pray as they wished, while subject populations in Christian lands had no official status whatever and no security beyond the king's pleasure. Some Christian monarchs, like Roger of Sicily, encouraged harmony and openness, and some Muslim rulers were harsh in their restriction of Christians, but the overall pattern clearly indicated that Islamic societies were much more consistent than their Christian neighbours in accommodating other faith communities in their midst. The enforced baptism of every subject of the Catholic kings of "reconquered" Spain and the wholesale expulsion of any conscientious objectors had no real counterpart in the Muslim world, although unscrupulous governors in need of scapegoats did occasionally instigate ugly communal riots. During the long centuries of their retreat from the Balkans, the Ottomans consistently offered asylum to European Jews fleeing from the pogroms of Russia and the capricious gestures of Western governments.

The tragic Armenian massacres would show how well the Turkish nationalists had learned the lesson of ethnic friction along with the rest of the curriculum of modernist statecraft. European attitudes to religious minorities were changing even before the Peace of Augsburg belatedly acknowledged the ruler's prerogative to choose the state church, and the toleration granted to dissident Christians was sooner or later extended to people of other faiths (or none). In today's secular democracies, a person's religion is a private matter with no immediate bearing on questions of domicile or employment. Muslims, like everyone else, live within the frame of a religiously neutral state, even though a few lingering regulations or customs give the Christians some vestiges of power or prestige. The newcomers have had to press for recognition of their special needs regarding times of prayer or places of ablution, but they have usually gained some satisfaction. Often, they have enjoyed the assistance of local Christians in their quest for fair treatment.

Shortly before the arrival of the Spaniards, Muslims founded a number of statelets on Mindanao and some smaller islands nearby. Four centuries later, the independent Republic of the Philippines is the only country in Asia with a Christian majority. The frustrations which Muslims there have encountered in their dealings with the Christian political authorities have induced some of them to resort to armed rebellion, while many others have sought to persuade the government to allow the Moro community sufficient autonomy for the fulfilment of religious duties. Here, as elsewhere, the situation has been complicated by ethnic and economic factors as well as by the shifts in policy which follow changes in leadership. Communal exasperation is more social than religious, as the chief opponents of any special arrangement have been secular representatives of the administration, while the principal voices of the churches have advocated a more conciliatory stance. Several interfaith groups — ranging from theological colloquia to juvenile athletic leagues — have endured through shootouts and standoffs alike.

In other parts of Asia, such historic Christian communions as the Assyrian, Malankara and Mar Thoma churches have survived relationships of varying intensity with their Muslim neighbours. Indeed, the Assyrians have been in a dialogue of necessity ever since the first Islamic century. More recently, missionaries from abroad have helped to launch many new churches which must now articulate Christian witness in their own cultural vocabularies. Several of these newer churches are in predominantly Muslim environments, but official attitudes towards them are by no means uniform. In Oman and most of the Gulf states, expatriate congregations pray without serious hindrance. Under the Shah, the Iranian government was generally tolerant as long its political interests were not challenged, but the Islamic Republic has been repressive to the point of assassinating clerics and executing all persons suspected of being apostates from Islam. Bangladesh has been the locus of a meek but persistent interfaith dialogue movement led by a prominent Muslim lawyer, and the contacts which it has realized offer some hope of developing into a network of solidarity as the nation seeks to establish its constitutional personality.

Two Islamic states in Asia have had notably difficult experiences in seeking a national consensus about the status of Christians and members of other minority faith groups. Pakistan owes its political existence to a sense of Islamic identity, and it is normal for a state founded by Muslims as an expression of their special legal and cultural heritage to enact *shari`ah* as the law of the land. Disagreement has arisen over the specific interpretations to adopt, and one important topic of controversy has been the role of *dhimmis* in the modern Islamic state. Such a subject has an impact far beyond paying taxes or holding worship services, for it touches such sensitive points as eligibility for parliamentary representation and ministerial, judicial or military positions, as well as personal credibility as a witness in courts of law, employment in the civil service or admission to certain academic institutions.

Christians in Malaysia, which became a multi-cultural, multi-faith society through intensive immigration during the British regime, have endured a range of annoyances from regulations on religious vocabulary to severe limitations on freedom of speech. There is a strong civil rights movement under Muslim leadership, but this has had scant success against the prevalent official attitude; indeed, its leaders have spent much time in jail with their Christian allies in a campaign for fair elections and an egalitarian society. On the other hand, it is ironic that Iraq has consistently enjoyed one of the best reputations in Islamic Asia for guaranteeing to its Christian citizens the same rights and privileges as their Muslim compatriots.

Like Malaysia, Fiji received many immigrants from southern Asia during the era of British imperial rule, so that by the time of independence the country's original population found itself surrounded by communities of different ethnic and religious backgrounds. Muslim and Hindu spokespersons sought alliances with rival groups within the (largely Methodist) Fijian political elite, but the suspension of parliamentary activity and the deterioration of social stability induced most of the non-Fijians to remove themselves to more congenial political climes. The problems were more ethnic than religious, but it is interesting to note that several Muslim leaders had argued that their co-religionists should be closer to the Fijian Christians than the Hindus, who may have shared some cultural and linguistic affinities but whose theology and cosmology set them at variance.

Egypt was the first country in Africa to have a Muslim government responsible for the well-being of a large number of Christian subjects. Successive Muslim dynasties, including the Shi'i Fatimis, left the Egyptian Christians (Copts) with considerable autonomy in their internal affairs, although Muslims enjoyed important economic, social and political advantages. Over centuries, so many Egyptians adopted Islam that the Christian subjects were reduced to minority status, while Arabic became the principal language of the country. Trouble has erupted on occasion, and there have been many instances of discrimination, but it has usually been possible for Coptic Christians to practise their faith and participate in national affairs. Whether a Christian could be president of Egypt is still a topic for theorists, but several Christians have held cabinet portfolios and parliamentary seats, as well as senior posts in the diplomatic corps and civil service. The most illustrious of these, Boutros Boutros-Ghali, became secretary general of the United Nations.

Respect and partnership

There is no compulsion in religion. Integrity has become distinct from error, so whoever disbelieves in idols and puts faith in God has grasped the firmest hold, unbreaking. And God is All-hearing, All-knowing (Q 2:256).

Call to the way of your Lord with wisdom and fine exhortation, and argue with them in the better way; surely your Lord knows best who has strayed from his path, as he knows who are guided (Q 16:125).

In many parts of West Africa, early Christian missionaries had to contend with the nefarious effects of the European slave trade, while the Muslim community in the Sahel grew steadily through the quiet witness of devout merchants. The puritan leaders of the resistance to colonial encroachment eventually consolidated Islamic political preponderance just in time for indirect rule. In East Africa, on the other hand, Muslims like the sultans of Zanzibar or Tippu Tib in Kisangani controlled the slave trade, and European economic interests joined the churches in opposing and ultimately stopping the raids. The contrast is stark enough; quiet piety or sincere solidarity can lay sturdy spiritual foundations, but enslavement gangs hinder the proclamation of any faith and raise major obstacles to intercommunal trust. The legacy of these early encounters has affected every state within the broad religious frontier zone that traverses Africa from the Bab al-Mandab and the Comoro Islands in the Indian Ocean to Cape Verde and the Grain Coast on the shores of the Atlantic.

Muslim majorities in Senegal and Mali have generally shown considerable tolerance towards their small but influential Christian communities, while Christians in such lands as Sierra Leone and Ivory Coast have demonstrated a similar benevolence. The prevailing attitude in most of West Africa is a continuing affirmation of a common cultural heritage and an abiding sense of family reaching across confessional lines of relatively recent provenance. The first president of Senegal, with a population that is nine-tenths Muslim, was the Christian Leopold Senghor; conversely, the people of Cameroun chose as their first leader Ahmadou Ahidjo, a member of the Muslim minority. These two presidents set an African precedent by resigning to allow persons from their respective religious majorities to assume office, but the foundations of intercommunal cooperation had been firmly laid and in the new era of political pluralism most parties in this region count both Christians and Muslims among their militants.

Tensions have persisted, however, and several misunderstandings between the faith groups have festered, especially over family law. The maintenance of harmony depends on developing contacts and collaboration between members of the different communities on a frank, open, constructive and collaborative plane. When a church is thought to be too close to a focal point of local Muslim devotions or a venerable mosque is thought to be in the way of a new chapel, local leaders will find an amicable solution only in the measure of their mutual goodwill, and this will depend on their recent record of trust and respect. West Africa's most salient example of the urgency of sound intercommunal contacts is Nigeria, where current rivalries and dubious myths feed the suspicions of each group about the other community and inhibit constructive dialogue. But the effort for understanding continues, and solid interfaith political alliances are gradually acquiring a cohesion which should nurture a vibrant multi-faith society.

In Zaïre, memories of the slave trade have dissipated during the struggle to secure a democratic constitution. The Muslim community has participated in this popular endeavour and presumably shares in the general aspiration for an end to corruption and the introduction of free elections. The first president of Tanzania, Julius Nyerere, arranged to be succeeded by Ali Hasan Mwinyi, as a gesture of intercommunal solidarity. In most of East Africa, Muslims have joined freely in the political process on equal terms with their Christian compatriots, although some sense of frustration has led a few Muslims, in Kenya for example, to form communal political parties to protect their own interests when these seem threatened by particular policies of the governments in office. Even in those countries where difficulties are more tenacious, African societies have tended to favour an open forum where Christians and Muslims can live as neighbours and all are free to choose and preach the faith which they prefer.

The movement for Indonesian independence was remarkable for the way in which it enhanced the mutual respect of the Muslims and Christians who worked side by side at every level on every front. The constitution recognizes both Roman Catholicism and Protestantism as official religions, along with Islam, Buddhism and Hinduism. This status is a mixed blessing, for it gives a pretext to those in authority who would regulate religious practice or impose an artificial conformity to political models of behaviour, but interference of this sort has provided opportunities for leaders of the various faith communities to articulate a common stand for toleration and free expression. Some Muslims have resented what they consider to be a disproportionate role in policy formation enjoyed by Christians, and some Christians have worried that their participation in political leadership has risked serious compromises of principle in such cases as the occupation of East Timor.

In the Caribbean, there are a number of states such as Trinidad and Guyana which received new populations from a broad range of confessional backgrounds. Muslims of Asian and African origin live in mixed communities with Christians, whose ancestries are even more diverse, and people of a great variety of other beliefs. In virtually all of these small states, Christians, Muslims and their fellow citizens form political alliances along lines of social or economic interest, so parties generally include persons from most religious groups. This observation is most valid in countries where political processes have been relatively free of corruption, but it also holds true in areas where sustained oppression has instigated the formation of popular fronts to rally the public against the abusers of power in the hope of introducing a new and fairer regime. Rare appeals to religious sensibilities, like the abortive coup in Trinidad, have usually led to a reaffirmation of the general sense of the common interest of all the populace.

Syncretism and supersession

> Say: O people of the Book, come to a common word between us and you, that we worship none but God, and that we associate naught with him, and that we do not take from among ourselves lords apart from God. And if they turn away, say: Bear witness that we are Muslims (Q 3:64).

> And when Jesus came with the clear signs he said: I have come to you with wisdom to make clear to you some of your differences, so fear God and obey me. God is surely my Lord and your Lord, so worship him; this is a straight path (Q 43:63f.).

Religious ideology has been as important as political and military tactics in the altercations between Muslims and Christians. Several passages of the Qur'an plainly assert that the Islam sent down to Muhammad was the same primal religion followed by Adam, Noah, Abraham and all the other prophets. An essential part of Muhammad's mission was, therefore, to correct the errors of the Jews and Christians, who had misunderstood or misinterpreted the messages entrusted to Moses and Jesus respectively. It was only a matter of time before all true worshippers would be guided to the true light of faith and become Muslims. The Qur'an quotes Jesus to this effect, indicating that even his most stubborn followers will understand their errors in doctrine on the Day of Judgment.

This confidence was reinforced by the relative ease of the Muslims' early military victories over the Byzantines and other Christian armies and further encouraged by the ready conversion of many of their new subjects. Weariness with internecine debates on Christology, the attraction of social and political advancement and a genuine appreciation of the simplicity of the new faith all played a role in these changes in allegiance, as did the occasional periods of rigorous discrimination and harsh persecution. The children of mixed marriages were always reared as Muslims, and the extreme penalties imposed on apostates prevented any possibility of even a trickle of converts in the opposite direction.

There may be no compulsion in religion, but there has been a strong tradition of enforced conformity which persists in our own times, so that those rare individuals who choose to adopt another faith have more often than not felt constrained to leave home and live in a country where a change of creed is not a cause for social exclusion, expropriation or even execution. In the Islamic Republic of Iran, many Christians and Baha'is have been killed for abandoning Islam, and several notorious accounts are in circulation about the ordeals endured by new Christians in Somalia, Pakistan and elsewhere. Muslims in these and other countries have protested against the apparent contradiction of murder for the sake of truth, preferring to trust in divine providence to arrange for judgment and punishment in due time and measure.

When they first encountered the challenge of Islam, Christian theologians tended to assume that it was yet another variant of the basic messianic religion which had, since the time of

Constantine, become the only faith to be politically and socially acceptable on a general scale. John of Damascus and other Christian writers thus described Islam along with the rival forms of Christianity which they considered to be heresies. Such a perspective fits rather neatly into a system which places Christianity at the pinnacle of religious truth, superseding Judaism, gnosticism and paganism, overcoming the injuries of its own schisms and the darkness of unbelief. Centuries of adversity have not altogether erased such thinking in the regions which came under Muslim rule, and an even more vigorous expectation of ultimate triumph has animated much of the Western missionary movement of the past two hundred years.

Having soon abandoned the idea that its new competitor was simply a heretical distortion of its own teaching, Christian apologetics had great difficulty in finding an appropriate category for Islam. It had emerged far too late in history and much too near the heartland of the Christian world to be grouped with all those presumably archaic religions which may have been at least partially adequate in pre-Christian eras or in areas where the full light of the gospel had not yet shone. The most facile explanation portrayed Islam as a diabolical diversion sent to tempt the spiritually frail, but such an hypothesis begs the central question of the incarnation and sidesteps the supposition that all have fallen short of the glory of God. Another common conclusion has been that (despite the awkward chronology) Islam was meant to be a first step in monotheism for some cultures and individuals not yet ready for the fuller truth — without addressing the obvious questions of how the Almighty would so distinguish among peoples and why the Lord of the entire universe would arbitrarily deny to some nations what was freely offered to others.

To circumvent dogmatic incompatibility and bridge the chasm of mutual anathema, some Muslims and Christians have sought formulas affirming the basic soundness of both faiths as imperfect expressions of human response to the majesty and mercy of God. Muslim versions of such theories tend to boil down to restatements of the classic teaching that since Islam did not differ from pristine Christianity true Christians would necessarily identify with traditional Islamic doctrine. Similarly, Christian attempts to admit Muhammad into the fellowship of the prophets have generally avoided the critical dilemmas posed by the evident discrepancies concerning Incarnation, Atonement and the Trinity. It may not be necessary or even possible to prove the ultimate truth of either faith in a categorically empirical fashion. Each generation of Christians and Muslims in every culture and society will have to respond to the circumstances which call them to live together in their differences. Some will try to force the others to conform to the official religion or at least seek to prevent any open expression of the other. Others will try hard to persuade their neighbours to forsake one set of beliefs and join the other camp — for their own good or for the benefit of the wider community. Still others will prefer to cloud real differences in a miasma of solidarity prone to collapse at the first test. Perhaps there is a more excellent way (1 Cor. 12:31).

Pluralism and peace

> O humankind! We created you from a male and a female, and we set you as peoples and tribes so that you might know one another. The noblest among you in the sight of God is the most pious of you. God is all-knowing, all-aware (Q 49:13).

> To you your religion, and to me my religion (Q 109:6).

Christian and Muslim communities now live together in virtually every part of the world. In a few countries, such as India, Israel and Sri Lanka, both are minorities, while in some, like Nigeria and Sudan, the two are nearly equal in numbers and far larger than any other group of believers. Wherever either is the dominant religious element, the other enjoys at least the formal right to follow its own paths of faith, except in Sa'udi Arabia, where Christian worship is still officially proscribed. The foregoing paragraphs have indicated how cautious and suspicious relations between Muslims and Christians have usually been, and it remains to consider current prospects for plural societies based on free association.

In countries which have adopted the constitutional framework of secular democracy, legal principles solemnly affirm the equal rights of all citizens, including freedom of worship. Provisions of this sort have generally sufficed for most Christian churches, but their guarantees are essentially passive or negative, and Muslims (along with other minorities) have often been frustrated in their quest for more positive recognition.

In Europe and North America, some statutes and a few labour contracts have assured access to appropriate facilities for ablutions and prayers in the workplace, and acknowledged the equal standing of Muslim festivals with Christian and Jewish holidays. Accommodation has been less spontaneous in more complex fields of law, notably with regard to families and the preparation of food. Many Christians have been reluctant to endorse these adjustments, fearing irreparable harm to the supposedly Christian heritage of the host societies. Deep cultural anxieties are bared when Muslims open *halal* shops or wear traditional clothes. The same forebodings, however, are voiced when Christians from eastern Europe or the Mediterranean ask to build new parish facilities, or when the leaders of ancient indigenous populations seek recognition for their spiritual objects and ceremonies. Curiously, these guardians of purity at home are often most critical of any presumed deficiency in cultures abroad.

Few political democracies are flourishing in Africa and Asia, but there is a growing company of partisans of some form of participatory government. Many Christians expect that parliamentary elections and a combination of customary law with civil and criminal codes adapted from Western models will furnish an adequate forum for modern political activity. But the principal weakness in this assumption lies in the presumed neutrality of the state, which for Muslims seems too susceptible to human manipulation — by Christians or anyone else who can marshall the requisite power. Furthermore, many Muslims may also perceive the intended religious neutrality as a militant secularism to be used against any spirituality at all. More than one European legislature has shown that this concern is not unfounded.

Another major focus of debate has been the place of Islamic *shari'ah* in the legal structure of the state. Muslim minorities want the right to administer their own laws regarding such family matters as marriage, divorce, child custody, inheritance and burials, but their claims are generally resisted by representatives of the Christian and secular majority, who prefer a uniform system which is easy to operate and which treats everyone on equal terms. In Islamic countries where some version of the *shari'ah* is part of the judicial fabric, Christian and other minority representatives express misgivings about rules of evidence (which may ascribe more force to the testimony of Muslims than to sworn statements from other witnesses, or even set a whole gradation of relative reliability based on gender and social status), the applicability to non-Muslims of certain prohibitions (pork, alcohol, usury) and penalties (lapidation, amputation) or official meddling in the affairs of supposedly autonomous and protected communities of faith.

Any contradictions are more apparent than real. Muslims generally follow the classical separation of religious communities. Thus, it is Muslims who would extend a particular version of the *shari'ah* to Muslim minorities, while other Muslims use their avowed respect for the *shari'ah* to justify the relegation of non-Muslims to inferiority. Whether they live in minority or majority communities, Christians generally advocate egalitarian and religiously neutral political and legal systems, and are thus unlikely to support any arrangement which sets them at a disadvantage or gives a privileged status for religious reasons to any group at all.

The only feasible agreement is to balance the principle of general application with a respect for particular communal concerns. The inclusion of the absolute values of the *shari'ah* in national codes and the disallowing of legislation inimical to the practice of Islam would in no way curtail the free exercise of Christian religion in the same society, as long as there is a clear constitutional guarantee that all citizens owe the same obligations of taxes and service to a government to which all have equal access, in which each has an equal right to participate and from which everyone can claim equal benefits. Christians in high office would fulfil the recognized criteria for rulers of Muslims, and Muslims in similar positions of authority would uphold the equal standing of Christians, Muslims and all other citizens. Details must vary according to local circumstances, but such a structure is permissible and practical wherever people of goodwill can find the necessary mutual trust and sense of common purpose.

9. An Agenda for Affection

The form and content of interaction between Muslims and Christians are set by the social and political currents in their particular contexts, the impact of events and personalities and the degree of mutual trust and understanding accrued. In some areas, minorities harbour an urgent concern about communal identity and basic religious freedom, while elsewhere people freely engage in open, equal exchange and act together in lawful and pacific collaboration. The pragmatic agenda is always the most urgent, and it remains an earnest obligation on all who claim to serve the God of peace and love to work tirelessly to ensure that every worshipper may perform religious duties unhindered by persecution or discrimination. Although even this is sometimes fraught with risks, there are people everywhere willing to build with their neighbours on a foundation of human dignity.

In more tranquil contexts, the programme will be more sober and deliberate, but no less serious. Perhaps the most pressing point of encounter centres on the rule of law and the possibility of accommodating the principles and procedures of *shari`ah* and *fiqh* with the codes and customs which Christians consider vital guarantors of all essential freedoms, including the observance of ritual requirements. Some anxiety haunts the very term *shari`ah*, and there is much to be said for a series of frank and constructive interfaith seminars on the plethora of interpretations of this concept and how it can be applied. In addition to judicial harmony, discussion of law may include rules of evidence, criteria of political eligibility, economic regulations related to interest and banks and such seemingly minor but really important topics as slaughtering animals and the proper burial of the dead.

Family law is in critical need of elucidation, because so many interfaith marriages join partners who lack the knowledge or incentive to inform their spouses of communal traditions. Most such unions occur with little encouragement from either religious establishment. The couples are optimistic, and in many cases their dedication and determination are successful, and their homes become authentic foyers of interfaith enhancement. Others, sadly, are unable to overcome the inevitable challenges facing any marriage — difficulties exacerbated by differences of custom at the very core of their relationship.

Many Christians consider matrimony a sacrament and most see it as a mutual commitment of one man and one woman. The idea of sacraments is quite foreign to Muslims, who generally understand marriage as a contractual arrangement susceptible to eventual dissolution. Muslim husbands may wish to enter polygamous unions, or they may decide to end their marriage. Wives unhappy with either course of action have scant means of resistance. Conversely, a woman wanting a divorce faces an elaborate process and must normally expect her children to be wards of their father. Another source of grievance lurks in differing expectations of inheritance, and many unpleasant surprises have deepened the distress of bereaved persons who might feel cheated by a system which they did not fully understand.

Preparation for interfaith marriage, neglected because the marriage is often unwelcome to relatives and religious leaders, is even more essential than the counselling usually given to prospective spouses from similar backgrounds. Rather than ignoring or simply denouncing a phenomenon which is becoming increasingly common in today's plural societies, leaders in both religious communities could share in developing appropriate materials to initiate the partners in mixed-faith unions to the special aspects of their situation. While general discussion of such curricula could take place in an international setting, the particular circumstances of each marriage would be well served by elaborating local approaches or, at the very least, establishing links between religious officials in multifaith communities to ensure adequate consultation in each instance. Besides weddings, common support for marriages in difficulty and joint ministry in times of bereavement fall within the ambit of these links, along with explorations towards a mutually acceptable system of inheritance.

One of the ecumenical meetings which prepared the ground for the World Council of Churches was the 1937 Life and Work conference in Oxford, whose theme was "Church, Community and State". The interdependency of this triad, long a prime concern to Muslims, is an important topic for interfaith consideration. Some aspects of this are so self-evident — such as opposition to apartheid and other forms of racism — that common action is virtually inescapable. Others areas of possible collaboration are exemplified by recent operations to transport medical supplies to war-torn countries and to work in support of human rights and on behalf of refugees. Discussions about relationships in the workplace — fair compensation for injuries and disabilities, facilities and time for prayers and fasts, allocation of a common rest day for families — can build respect and trust even as they develop programmes of general benefit. Interfaith conversations about economic problems like debt and the roles of public and private agencies (including governments, cooperatives, trade unions, transnational corporations and international regulatory bodies) in determining the evolution of structure and policy would be instructive to all participants and conducive to financial stability and communal harmony.

That the Arabic words for "creation" (*khalq*) and "ethics" (*akhlaq*) derive from the same root suggests that human society bears a moral responsibility for the integrity of the *oikoumene*. Muslims and Christians can help each other towards a fuller appreciation and acceptance of their shared obligations by examining together the complex balance of order and authority, including the influence religious leaders might have on the conduct of the faithful and the mechanisms for establishing and articulating consensus within and among various communities. Exchanges about sexual ethics and gender role models can help to dissipate unfair stereotypes and stimulate useful reflections on the continuity and adaptation of values and customs in every quarter. Human intervention in nature and our privileges and duties as God's representatives and partners in creation underlie another critical area of common endeavour.

Awareness of our failures as keepers of the ecosystem may be of comparatively recent provenance, but it is a corollary of the shortcomings recognized in the theme of the World Council of Churches' first assembly (Amsterdam 1948) — "Man's disorder and God's design". Here is another subject which has long engaged the attention of pious Muslims and which, therefore, holds the promise of a fruitful bilateral exploration. After centuries of separate experimentation in fashioning human societies to conform to the kingdom of God, Christians and Muslims may be approaching a threshold leading to new social systems that will help believers to grow spiritually as individuals, in their own traditions and through the mutual enrichment of reciprocal esteem.

A shared perspective on our stewardship is increasingly imperative as scientists create new dilemmas for our consciences. Many innovations touch our very nature. From nuclear fission to genetic engineering and beyond, each of these holds immense potential for good or harm, leaving human agents with the awesome power to improve the quality of earthly life or to inflict suffering on fellow-humans and the other denizens of God's universe. People who profess to serve a merciful God and those who proclaim the greatest virtue to be *agapé* or loving solidarity with all one's neighbours have common cause in the vigilant defence of responsible freedom and advocacy for the weak and vulnerable. Even though deep disagreements may occur on particular issues, prayerful perseverance will enable the emergence of conciliatory viewpoints or at the very least a mutual understanding of the differences.

One further common focus of Muslim and Christian faith perspectives is the peace of God which Muslims wish upon everyone they meet. Various perceptions of peace in different traditions and in the hearts of individual believers could lead us to a dialogue about spirituality which would sharpen insights and broaden horizons. An appreciation of how others have considered such theological puzzles as the balance between reason and revelation or the apparent rivalry between the sovereignty of God and human autonomy can add surprising dimensions to our own understanding of the same questions. Mystics in the two communities have long shared a spiritual vocabulary and followed parallel itineraries, but we need not be experts in esoteric exercises to deepen our acquaintance with God through conversations with other worshippers.

A relatively simple motif for beginners could be the notion of vocation or call, both in terms of how we sense God's call in our lives and try to share it with our neighbours (*da`wah*) and how we formulate our appeals or petitions to the Almighty (*du`ah*). Some pioneering ventures in common study of the Bible and the Qur'an indicate that a rich harvest awaits those who would invest the requisite spiritual energy. Related points include the roles of scripture and tradition in setting doctrinal norms, the importance of judgment and the last day in our faith journeys and the whole problematic of developing a theology of pluralism. We can learn from our experiences and from the accounts of our partners, and a stronger sense of interdependence may well bring many Muslims to join with their Christian friends in the prayerful theme of the WCC's 1991 assembly in Canberra: "Come, Holy Spirit — renew the whole creation!"

There is thus no shortage of topics for serious consideration by Christians and Muslims together. How these common efforts are realized is as important as the actual subjects discussed. Activities on behalf of refugees or war victims should ordinarily be directed cooperatively, or a coalition of organizations could coordinate successive projects. This principle also applies to less urgent discussions and local projects like well-digging, concerts or athletic events. The primary concern is to encourage genuine partnership and dispel the risk or appearance of manipulation of the situation by any particular group. However, when one community is manifestly better equipped to undertake administrative detail, its leaders should proceed in full awareness of the real advantages in consulting partners in the fullest measure possible.

Whether members of different faith groups should join in common prayer will be best assessed by the participants in any encounter. It should be borne in mind that important contrasts have developed between the forms of prayer familiar to Christians and Muslims, and most attempts to fuse elements from both into a composite ceremony have commended themselves to relatively few observers. For some years now, the Pontifical Council for Interfaith Dialogue has sponsored an annual gathering of religious leaders at Assisi, where persons follow the rites of their respective faiths in the reverent presence of the others. Such a device affirms a sense of common petition in a structure which assures that worshippers are satisfied with the ritual framework of their supplications. To open less formal meetings, or to mark the initiation of any shared endeavour, the simplest expedient is for all to hear representatives of each community offer suitable prayers or readings.

Formal contacts between worldwide Muslim and Christian organizations have been growing in number and intensity in recent years. These links, involving the Pontifical Council for Interfaith Dialogue, the World Council of Churches, the World

Muslim League, the World Muslim Congress and similar bodies, reflect the common commitment of these institutions to consultation and harmony. Parallel exchanges have developed between regional and national institutions in several parts of the world, notably in Europe, where they have nurtured one of the few glimmers of hope in the maelstrom of the former Yugoslavia. Institutional contacts like these maintain vital networks of communication even as they give critical endorsement to the idea of peaceful collaboration and encourage regional and global interfaith groups to greater vigour in their quest for reconciliation and harmony.

To change our world, however, institutions will not suffice. To have any real possibility of ending the vicious cycle of suspicion and hostility which has poisoned relations between the Christian and Muslim communities for so long, individuals of goodwill must take an active part in removing obstacles and building relationships wherever they live. Superficial courtesy may well be a necessary first step, but it will prove idle and naive if it does not quickly develop into a profound solidarity conducive to earnest explanation and examination of the issues which beset our sisters and brothers in diverse circumstances around the globe. Pastors and imams, as well as religious bureaucrats in their several offices, can contribute enormously through teaching and example, but the vanguard of this holy campaign for peace will number the believers in both camps who take the serious spiritual risk of reaching out to their neighbours in prayerful determination to learn and build together. As citizens of a global village, we cannot avoid our common future; nor can we escape judgment on our actions and our inaction, our abuses and our graces.

Youth meetings, women's forums, professional gatherings of lawyers or educators or editors — every opportunity to reduce prejudice and stimulate understanding should be pursued with enthusiasm. Some countries are fortunate enough to have only minor social difficulties to discuss, while in other areas prospects of the most elementary co-operation seem beyond reasonable hope. Yet neither desperate resignation nor polite insularity is a likely foundation for practical collaboration. Institutional networks are essential to spreading information and sharing concern between places and between believers, but the vital objective to be pursued by everyone everywhere is a cogent and coherent social order which guarantees freedom and dignity to all. Patience, vigilance and sincerity are not abstract qualities but ethical imperatives incumbent on Muslims and Christians alike in our response to the call for justice, mercy and peace which we have all heard. The future is our awesome responsibility.

> Perhaps God will place affection between you and those whom you now consider to be enemies. God is all-powerful, all-merciful (Q 60:7).

> Humankind! We created you from a male and a female and we made you into nations and tribes so that you could get to know one another. Surely the most honourable among you before God is the one who is most pious. God is all-knowing and acquainted with all (Q 49:13).

> Let us pursue what makes for peace and for mutual upbuilding (Romans 14:19).

Amen.